T0321212

I am the Self, O Arjun, seated in the hearts of all creatures.
I am the beginning, the middle and the end of all beings.

~ Chapter 10, Verse 20, Bhagavad Gita

Published 2024

FiNGERPRINT!

An imprint of Prakash Books India Pvt. Ltd

113/A, Darya Ganj,
New Delhi-110 002
Email: info@prakashbooks.com/sales@prakashbooks.com

 Fingerprint Publishing
 @FingerprintP
 @fingerprintpublishingbooks
www.fingerprintpublishing.com

For manuscript submissions, e-mail: fingerprintsubmissions@gmail.com

ISBN: 978-93-5440-291-3

un
MIND

a graphic guide to Self-realization

Written by Siddharth Tripathi
Illustrated by Kalyani S Naravane

Based on the teachings of
Sri Ramana Maharshi & Sri Ramesh Balsekar

Introduction

Ken Wilber describes Sri Ramana Maharshi (1879 - 1950) as the 'greatest sage of this century and, arguably, the greatest spiritual realization of this or any time'. Maharshi's teachings carry tremendous spiritual strength; a few lines from him are enough for a ripe soul to attain Self-realization. He recommended the practice of Self-enquiry, which for many seekers, remains one of the most effective methods to attain enlightenment.

Ramesh Balsekar (1917-2009) was influenced by two spiritual giants — Sri Nisargadatta Maharaj and Sri Ramana Maharshi. Ramesh codified Advaita wisdom in a manner that answers many questions that modern seekers struggle with. His teachings put emphasis on non-doership as the key to understanding the Self.

My spiritual journey found its shore when I discovered the teachings of Sri Ramana Maharshi and Sri Ramesh Balsekar. I believe bringing the spiritual insights of these two masters in an accessible, visual format can be of great benefit to the serious seeker.

All human pursuit is born out of a longing for happiness (or peace of mind*). But we invariably attach conditions to this happiness — I'll be happy when I get a million dollars, or, I need to change jobs to be content, or, I am at peace when I'm in the hills alone, and so on. We keep hoping for an event or a change that'll make us happy. And there are times when we find happiness, but these are, sadly, only

These two terms are interchangeable. If you have peace of mind then you are happy, if you are happy you have peace of mind. Having uninterrupted peace of mind is being enlightened or Self-realized.

temporary conditions, bound by time and place — inevitably followed by frustration and pain.

Is that how it's supposed to be? Is there a way to lasting peace?
If one asked this question to an enlightened sage like Sri Ramana Maharshi or Ramesh Balsekar, their response would be, 'Yes, there is a way out, but to get there you must first find out who you really are'.

Who am I?
We rarely ask ourselves this question and even if we do, very few turn inward to seek the answer. The gurus simply point out that we haven't looked in the right direction; that if we turned inward and looked for ourselves, it would lead to Self-realization. There is no need for years of prayer and meditation, in fact there is no need to do anything at all. Just this knowledge once experienced leads to complete peace of mind.

However, it's not as easy as it appears to be. A significant part of the teachings go against everything you believe in and hence, you'll find them intriguing but hard to accept. Eventually, your personal experience and reflection will enable you to truly understand what the masters had to say.

We hope this book is able to plant a tiny seed of understanding that helps with your seeking.

PART 1

THE GRAND ILLUSION

1.

WAKEY, WAKEY, RISE AND SHINE

MONDAY. I woke up at 3 am. It was too early even for me.

I will feel drowsy through the day if I don't go back to sleep now...

I tried but couldn't get back to sleep. I shut my eyes and tried again.

ARGHHHHHHHHH!

I was awake when the alarm rang.

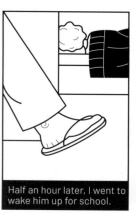

Half an hour later, I went to wake him up for school.

He was drooling on his pillow, sound asleep.

I was nice. I gave him a generous five minutes of wakey-wakey time. He asked for another five.

I got pissed. Arms taut, fingers pointed, I said...

GET UP!

10

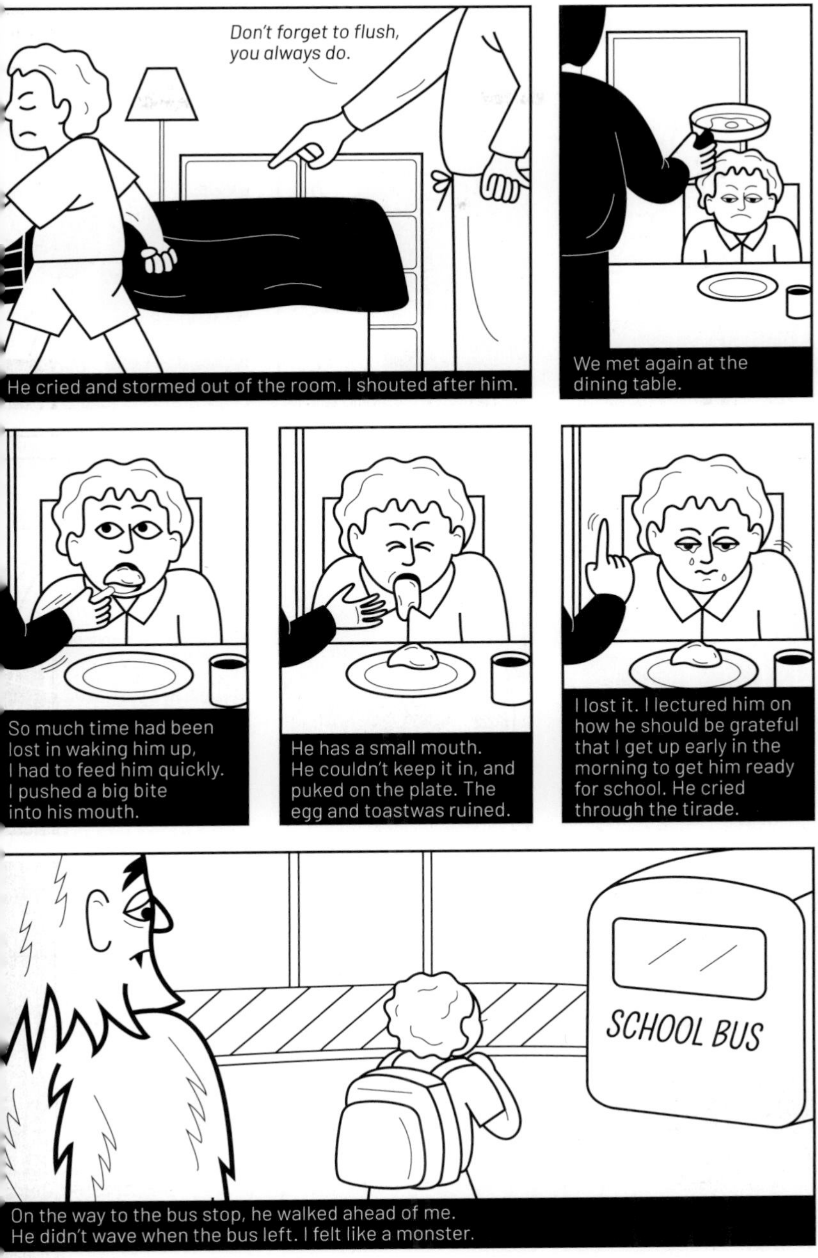
Don't forget to flush,
you always do.
He cried and stormed out of the room. I shouted after him.
We met again at the
dining table.
So much time had been
lost in waking him up,
I had to feed him quickly.
I pushed a big bite
into his mouth.
He has a small mouth.
He couldn't keep it in, and
puked on the plate. The
egg and toastwas ruined.
I lost it. I lectured him on
how he should be grateful
that I get up early in the
morning to get him ready
for school. He cried
through the tirade.
SCHOOL BUS
On the way to the bus stop, he walked ahead of me.
He didn't wave when the bus left. I felt like a monster.

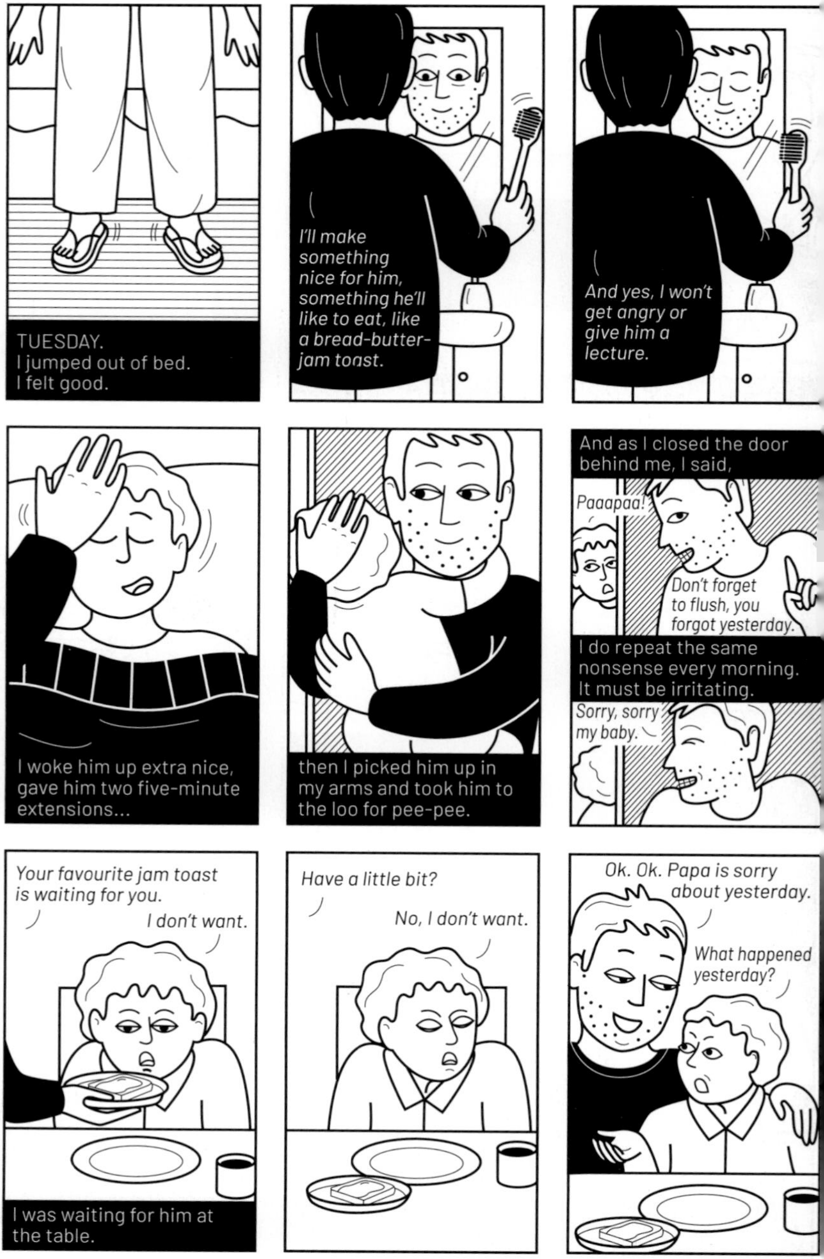
TUESDAY.
I jumped out of bed.
I felt good.
I'll make something nice for him, something he'll like to eat, like a bread-butter-jam toast.
And yes, I won't get angry or give him a lecture.
I woke him up extra nice, gave him two five-minute extensions...
then I picked him up in my arms and took him to the loo for pee-pee.
And as I closed the door behind me, I said,
Paaapaa!
Don't forget to flush, you forgot yesterday.
I do repeat the same nonsense every morning. It must be irritating.
Sorry, sorry my baby.
Your favourite jam toast is waiting for you.
I don't want.
I was waiting for him at the table.
Have a little bit?
No, I don't want.
Ok. Ok. Papa is sorry about yesterday.
What happened yesterday?

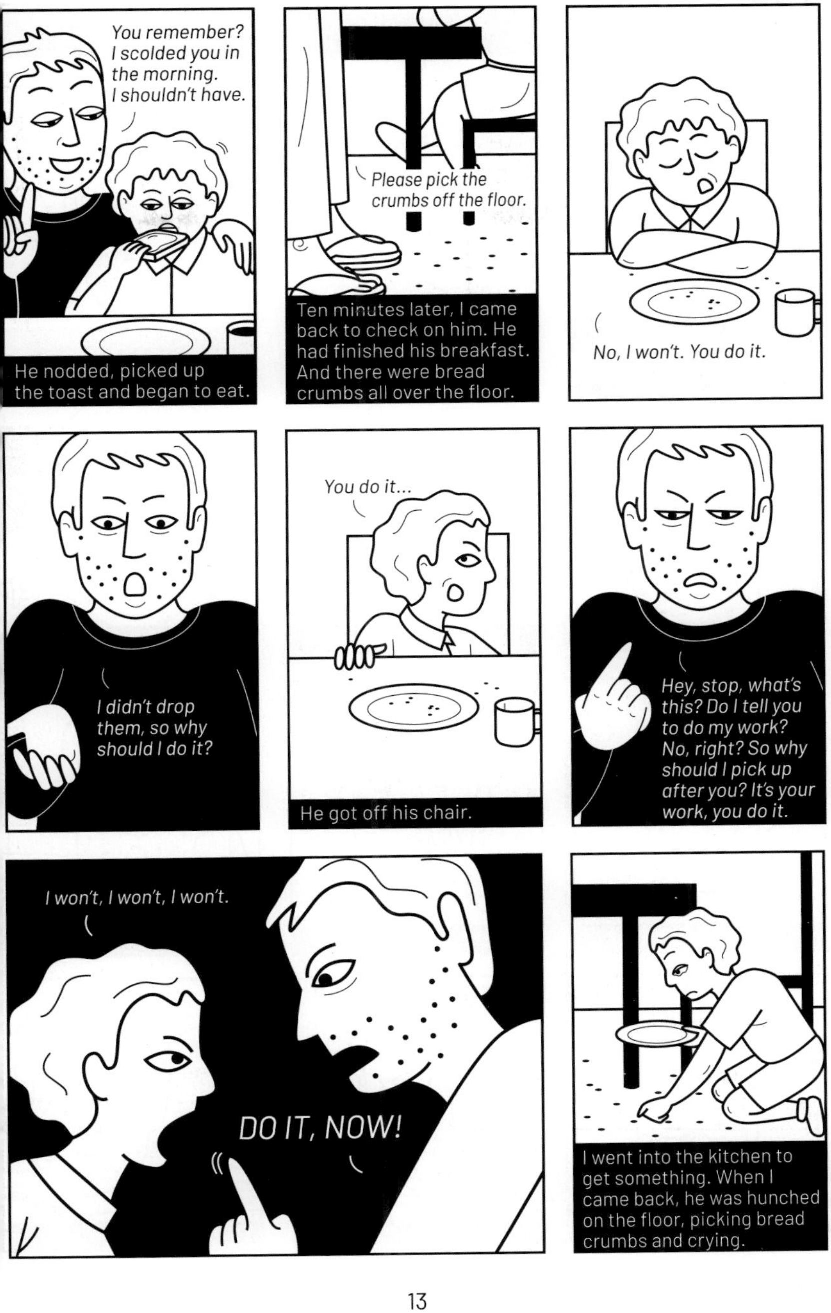

You remember? I scolded you in the morning. I shouldn't have.
He nodded, picked up the toast and began to eat.
Please pick the crumbs off the floor.
Ten minutes later, I came back to check on him. He had finished his breakfast. And there were bread crumbs all over the floor.
No, I won't. You do it.
I didn't drop them, so why should I do it?
You do it...
He got off his chair.
Hey, stop, what's this? Do I tell you to do my work? No, right? So why should I pick up after you? It's your work, you do it.
I won't, I won't, I won't.
DO IT, NOW!
I went into the kitchen to get something. When I came back, he was hunched on the floor, picking bread crumbs and crying.

Yes, my parenting is flawed, but there is an even more fundamental pattern that's staring at us here.

'I' woke up.

'I' couldn't go back to sleep.

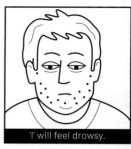

'I' will feel drowsy.

'I' shut my eyes and tried again.

The sound annoyed me (I).

'I' was nice.

'I' lost it.

'I' shouted after him.

'I' lectured him.

'I' scolded you.

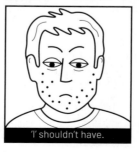

'I' shouldn't have.

'I' had made that egg.

Why should 'I' pick up after you?

Do 'I' tell you to do my work?

'I' was waiting.

'I' won't. 'I' won't. 'I' won't.

You (I) do it.

'I' felt like a monster.

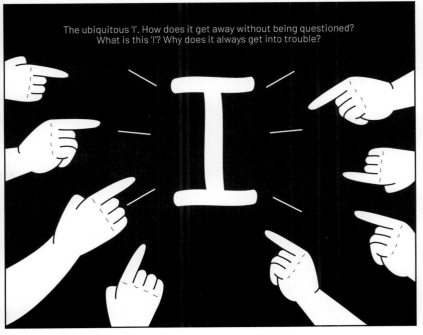

The ubiquitous 'I'. How does it get away without being questioned?
What is this 'I'? Why does it always get into trouble?

2.

THE RAMANA MAHARSHI ANSWER GENERATOR

All through the day
I me mine, I me mine, I me mine.

~ *I Me Mine*, **The Beatles**

The 'I' vacillates between the past and the future and there is no peace to be found with it around.

Past –
• If only 'I' had studied in college...
• If 'she' (the 'I' of another person) hadn't broken 'my' heart...

Future –
• My 'boss' will fire me if 'I' don't finish this assignment on time...
• Who will look after 'me' when 'I' get old...

Ramana Maharshi taught us to observe the pattern of this 'I'. According to him, if we could see through the falsehood of this 'I' and go beyond it, we could attain complete peace of mind.

In Ramana's peaceful presence, his devotees felt free to ask anything – sometimes the questions were weird and unrelated to his teaching. Ramana, with compassion and unwavering focus, brought them back to the real question (and to the essence of the teaching).

Isn't the power to turn invisible a sign of sainthood?

Visibility and invisibility refer to him who sees. Who is that?

Solve that question first. Other questions are unimportant.

What are the powers of supermen?

Whether the powers are high or low, they exist only with reference to him who possesses them.

Find out who that is.

Do we go to heaven as a result of our actions here?

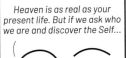

Heaven is as real as your present life. But if we ask who we are and discover the Self...

...what is the need to think about heaven?

Doubts keep arising. What should be done about it?

A doubt arises and it is cleared. Another arises and that is cleared too, only to make way for another, and it goes on. It is not possible to clear all doubts.

Find out instead to whom the doubts arise. Go to their source and stay there. Then they cease to arise. That is how doubts are to be cleared away.

3.

TWO QUESTIONS
ONE ANSWER

Hey! Come back and do your homework...

Venkataraman was the strong and sporty kind, always keen on games and mischief but not too gung-ho about studying. He lived with his uncle in Madurai (a town in Tamil Nadu, India).

One day, sometime mid-July, Venkataraman was sitting alone in a room on the first floor of his uncle's house.

Suddenly, he felt a sensation that filled him with fear. He felt as if he was going to die.

He wasn't sure why it was happening but the feeling was unmistakable.

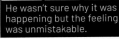

He didn't shout for help. It didn't even occur to him that he should tell someone about it.

He had decided to get to the bottom of this feeling on his own.

The shock and the fear drove his mind inwards.

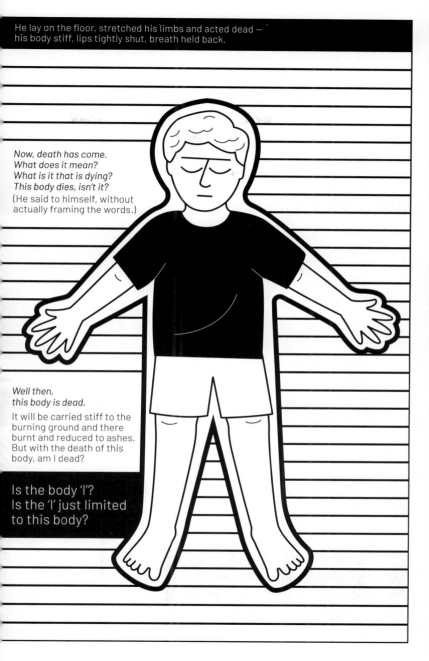

He lay on the floor, stretched his limbs and acted dead — his body stiff, lips tightly shut, breath held back.

Now, death has come.
What does it mean?
What is it that is dying?
This body dies, isn't it?
(He said to himself, without actually framing the words.)

Well then,
this body is dead.

It will be carried stiff to the burning ground and there burnt and reduced to ashes. But with the death of this body, am I dead?

Is the body 'I'?
Is the 'I' just limited to this body?

23

The realization came to him like a flash. The ego was lost in a flood of Self-awareness and the sixteen-year-old found himself on the peak of spirituality.

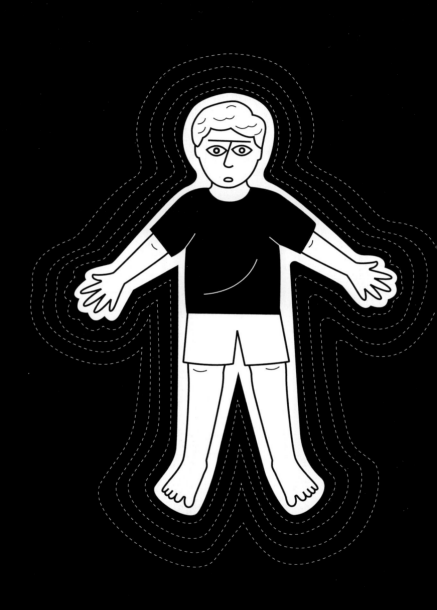

Venkataraman later on came to be known
as Bhagavan Sri Ramana Maharshi.

50 YEARS LATER

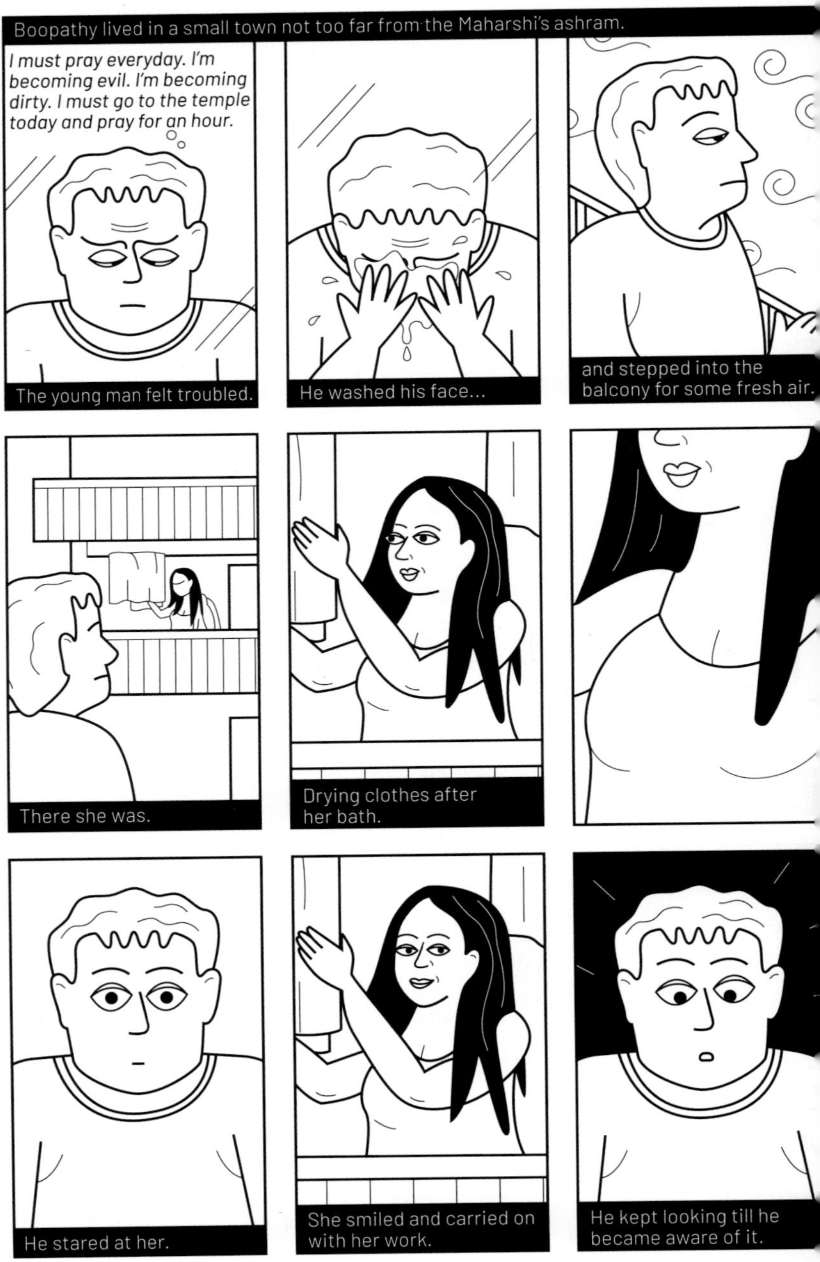
Boopathy lived in a small town not too far from the Maharshi's ashram.
I must pray everyday. I'm becoming evil. I'm becoming dirty. I must go to the temple today and pray for an hour.
The young man felt troubled.
He washed his face...
and stepped into the balcony for some fresh air.
There she was.
Drying clothes after her bath.
He stared at her.
She smiled and carried on with her work.
He kept looking till he became aware of it.

He shook his head in dismay...

Aye Boopathy, where are you going? Eat something before you go! Why are you in such a rush?

and ran down the stairs and out of the house. His mother shouted after him but he didn't stop.

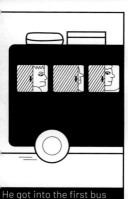

He got into the first bus to Tiruvannamalai.

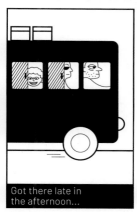

Got there late in the afternoon...

And went straight to the ashram.

The Maharshi was sitting in a small hall.

The young man went up to him and sat down beside him.

A few minutes later, the Maharshi opened his eyes, his gentle gaze fell upon the young man.

29

Ask, ask your question.

Someone whispered to him from the back.

I am carried away by the body of a young woman neighbour and I'm often tempted to commit adultery. What should I do?

He blurted out.

The Maharshi's kind eyes didn't judge.

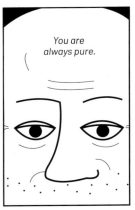

You are always pure.

It is your senses and your body that tempt you and which you confuse with your real self.

So first know who is tempted and who is there to tempt.

This doesn't sound like a moral lesson.

The young man nodded slowly.

But even if adultery is committed, do not think of it afterwards because you are always pure.

The Maharshi added...

You are not the sinner.

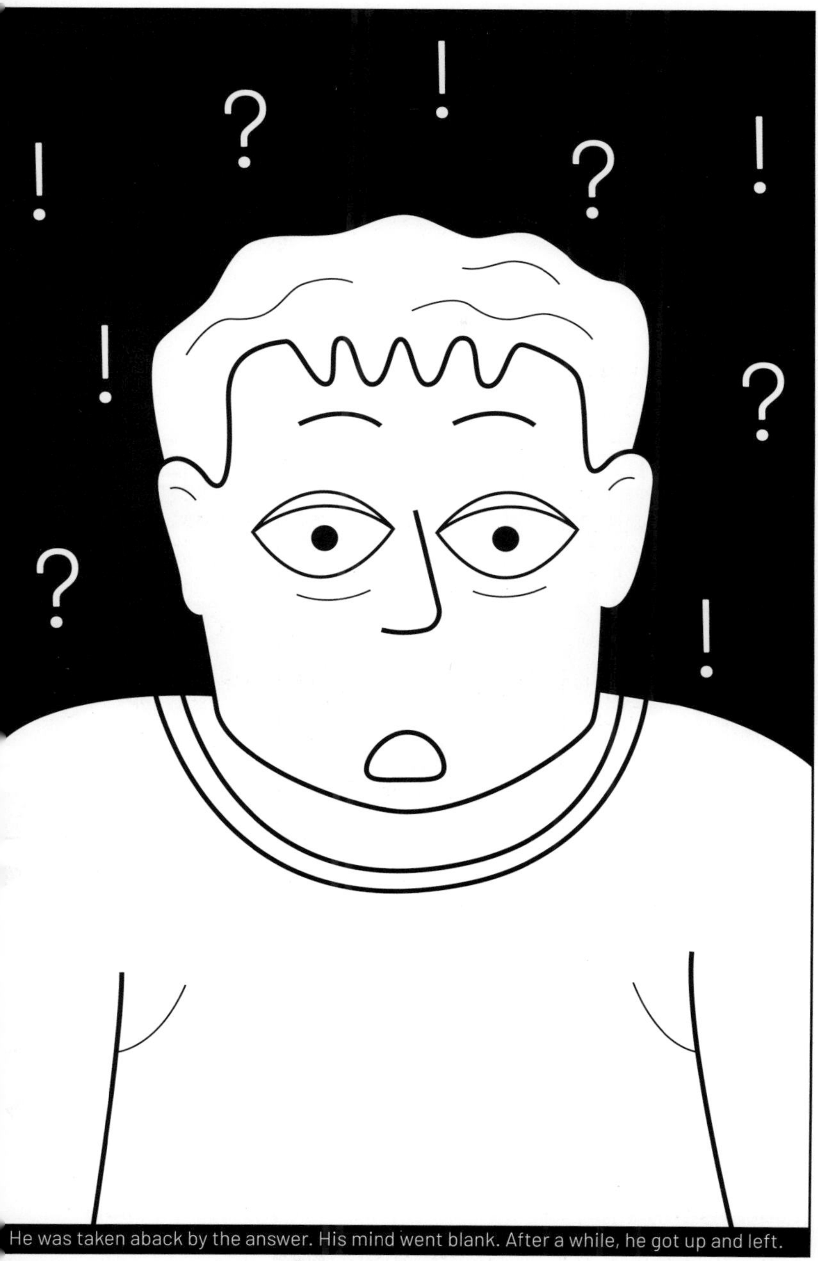
He was taken aback by the answer. His mind went blank. After a while, he got up and left.

How can he say I'm pure even if I commit adultery? It doesn't make any sense.

But for some reason, I know it to be true. Does it exonerate me from my feelings of lust? Is that why I believe it to be true? No, it's not that. Something inside me knows it to be true although my mind doesn't accept it.

You are always pure.

The words remained stuck in his head.

4.

SYMPATHY FOR
THE TOASTER

According to Sri Ramana, turning inward to find the 'I' and then going to its source is the path to Self-realization. For most of us, understanding the 'I', can be complex. Here's an example that Ramesh Balsekar used to illustrate this.

A toaster is a complex machine. It has

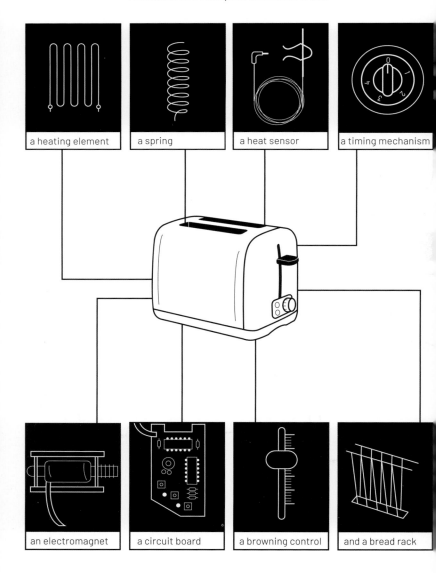

a heating element

a spring

a heat sensor

a timing mechanism

an electromagnet

a circuit board

a browning control

and a bread rack

Plug it into an
electric socket.

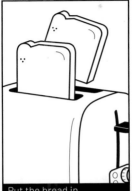

Put the bread in.

Set the dial to the
browning you need.

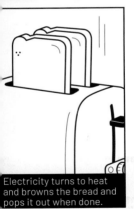

Electricity turns to heat
and browns the bread and
pops it out when done.

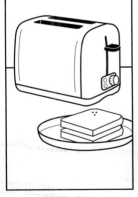

My toaster has been with
me for quite a number of
years. It had been a
competent, unassuming
device.

But then something extraordinary happened.

One day, the machine got an eye, an ear, a nose, and a central system to operate and interpret the signals coming from these new add-ons (let's call it the toaster's 'intellect').

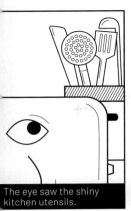

The eye saw the shiny kitchen utensils.

The ear heard people talking and laughing.

The nose could smell a burnt toast.

With the senses doing their job, thoughts couldn't be far behind.

The machine got its first thought.

Guess, what it could be?

It was the 'I', after all, there has to be someone who sees, smells, hears.

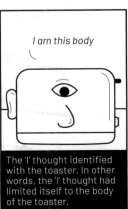

I am this body

The 'I' thought identified with the toaster. In other words, the 'I' thought had limited itself to the body of the toaster.

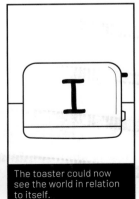

The toaster could now see the world in relation to itself.

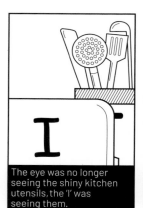

The eye was no longer seeing the shiny kitchen utensils, the 'I' was seeing them.
I
The ear was no longer hearing people talk, the 'I' was hearing them.
I
The nose no longer smelt the burnt toast, the 'I' smelt it.
I
That done, more thoughts could arise.
SOUND
SMELL
SHINY
BRIGHT
BROWN
BURNT
The toaster came up with words to express these thoughts.
A few weeks passed; the toaster had made a picture of who it could be.
I'm still and cold.
I'm white.
At times, something is put inside of 'me' and my lever is pushed down.

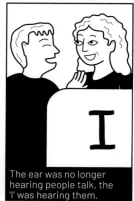

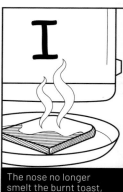

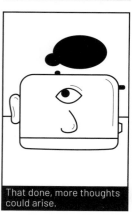

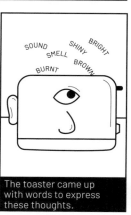

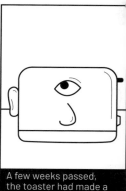

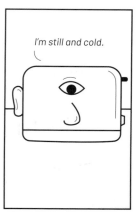

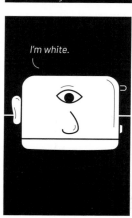

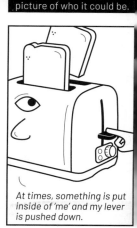

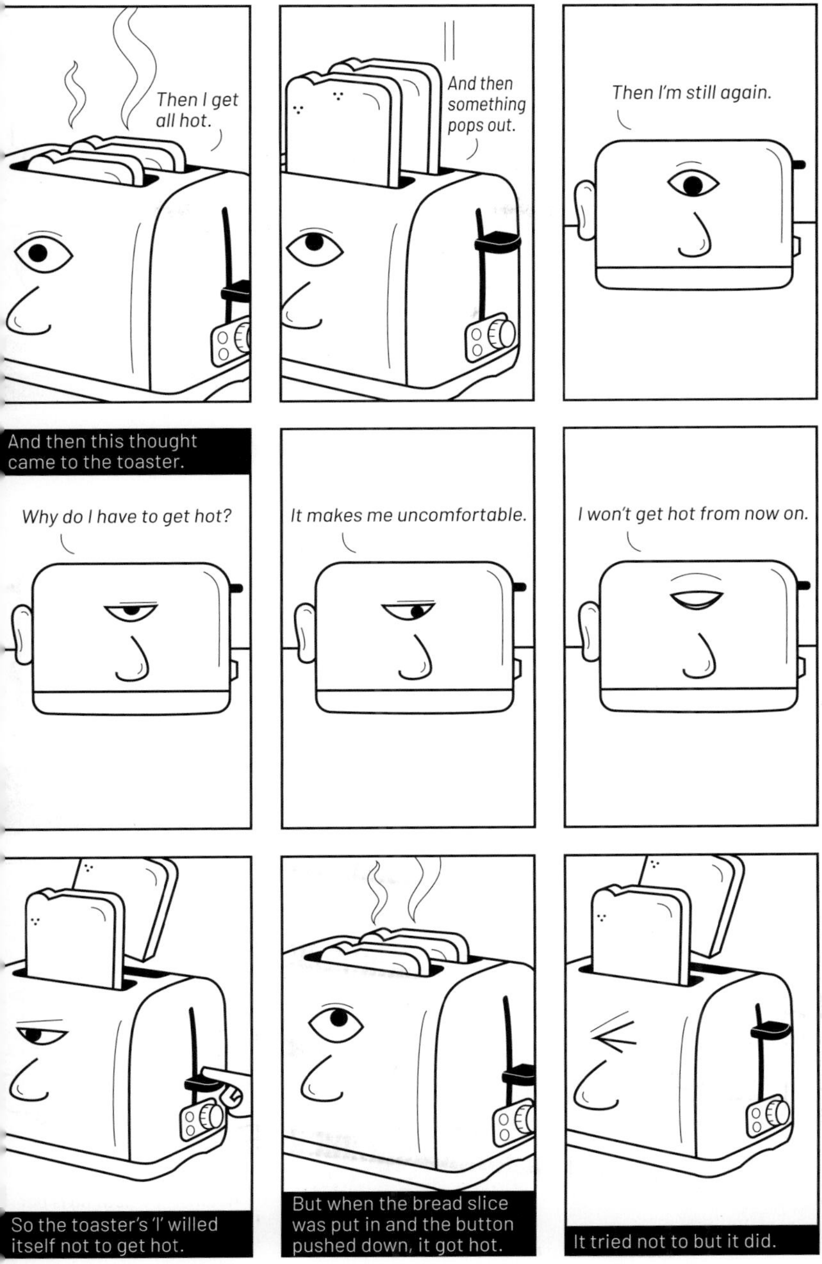
Then I get all hot.
And then something pops out.
Then I'm still again.
And then this thought came to the toaster.
Why do I have to get hot?
It makes me uncomfortable.
I won't get hot from now on.
So the toaster's 'I' willed itself not to get hot.
But when the bread slice was put in and the button pushed down, it got hot.
It tried not to but it did.

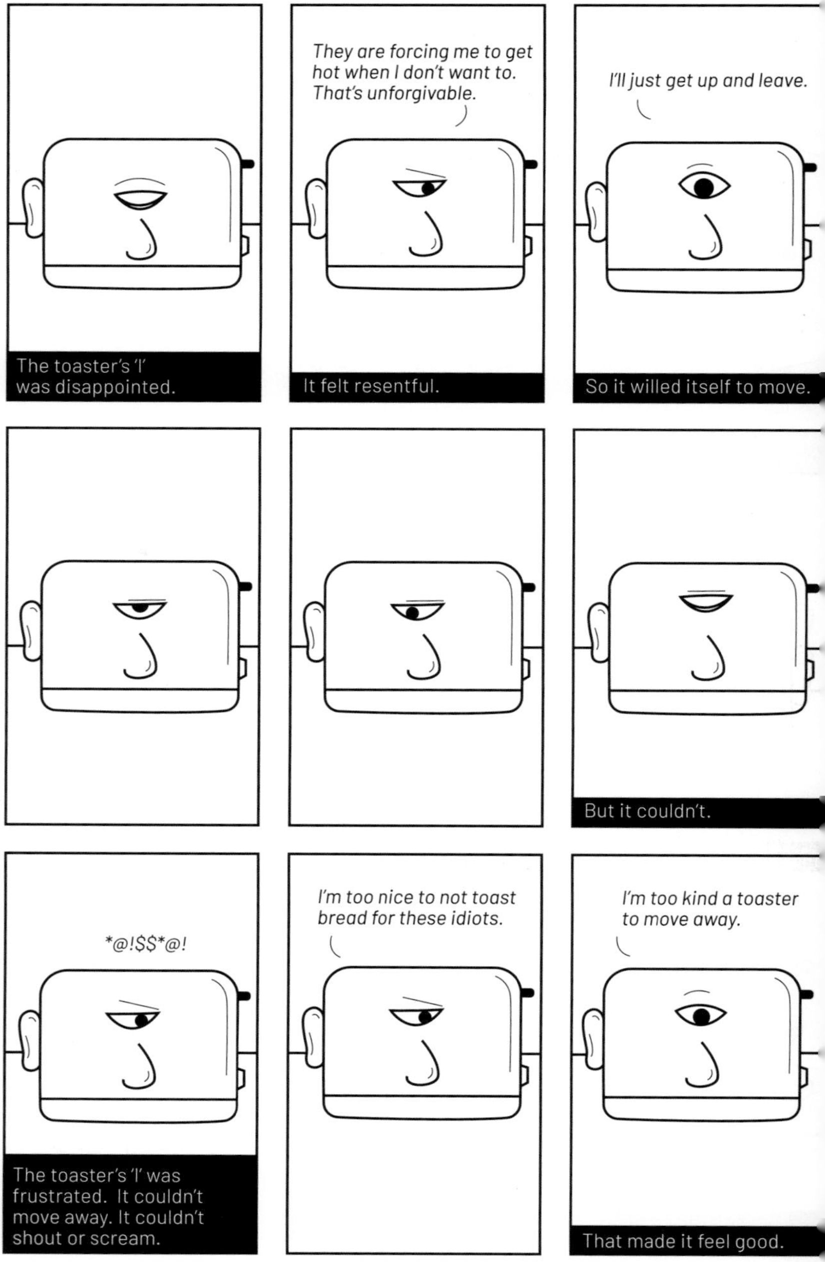
The toaster's 'I' was disappointed.
They are forcing me to get hot when I don't want to. That's unforgivable.
It felt resentful.
I'll just get up and leave.
So it willed itself to move.
But it couldn't.
@!$$@!
The toaster's 'I' was frustrated. It couldn't move away. It couldn't shout or scream.
I'm too nice to not toast bread for these idiots.
I'm too kind a toaster to move away.
That made it feel good.

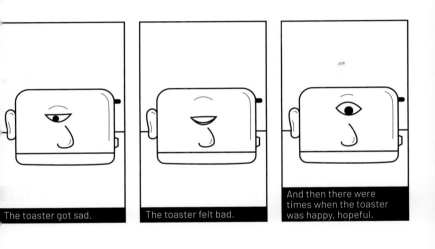

The toaster got sad.

The toaster felt bad.

And then there were times when the toaster was happy, hopeful.

And so it goes.

The toaster's intellect interacts with the senses (hearing, sight, smell, etc.); the senses provide the intellect (mind) with impressions of the world and based on these impressions the intellect forms an identity 'I'. The 'I' constitutes the body of the toaster and its mind (or intellect). The 'I' limits itself to this body-mind complex. Anything that's not this 'I' becomes the 'other'. The toaster's 'I' assumes that it is doing things/can do things, for example, it is toasting bread, it can run away if it wants.

In reality, the 'I' is just a thought. The 'I' does nothing. It takes ownership for what the toaster's pre-programmed functionality is doing and gets frustrated when it isn't able to run away ('running' is something that the toaster isn't programmed to do).

The same applies to human beings. All our resentment and anxiety is like that of the toaster — at our inability to change people or events, at our inability to change ourselves.

So there it is, the 'I' is an imaginary concept (the mind identifying with the body and creating the concept of 'I'). It is a thought (the first thought) that all other thoughts rely on for their origin, that is, if there was no 'I' then other thoughts can't occur since all thoughts are in relation to the 'I' and the 'other' (the world).

18.

Thoughts alone make up the mind;
And of all thoughts, the 'I' thought is the root.
What is called mind is but the notion 'I'.

19.

When one turns within and searches
The shamed 'I' vanishes
And wisdom's quest begins.

~ Verse 18 & 19, Upadesa Saram, Sri Ramana Maharshi

Turning inward to find one's true Self (and not the illusory 'I') is the path recommended by the Maharshi. But for that to happen, the mind's 'I' needs to weaken its hold, that is, the ego needs to go. This can be achieved to a large extent by understanding how human beings really operate.

(Hint: somewhat like the toaster.)

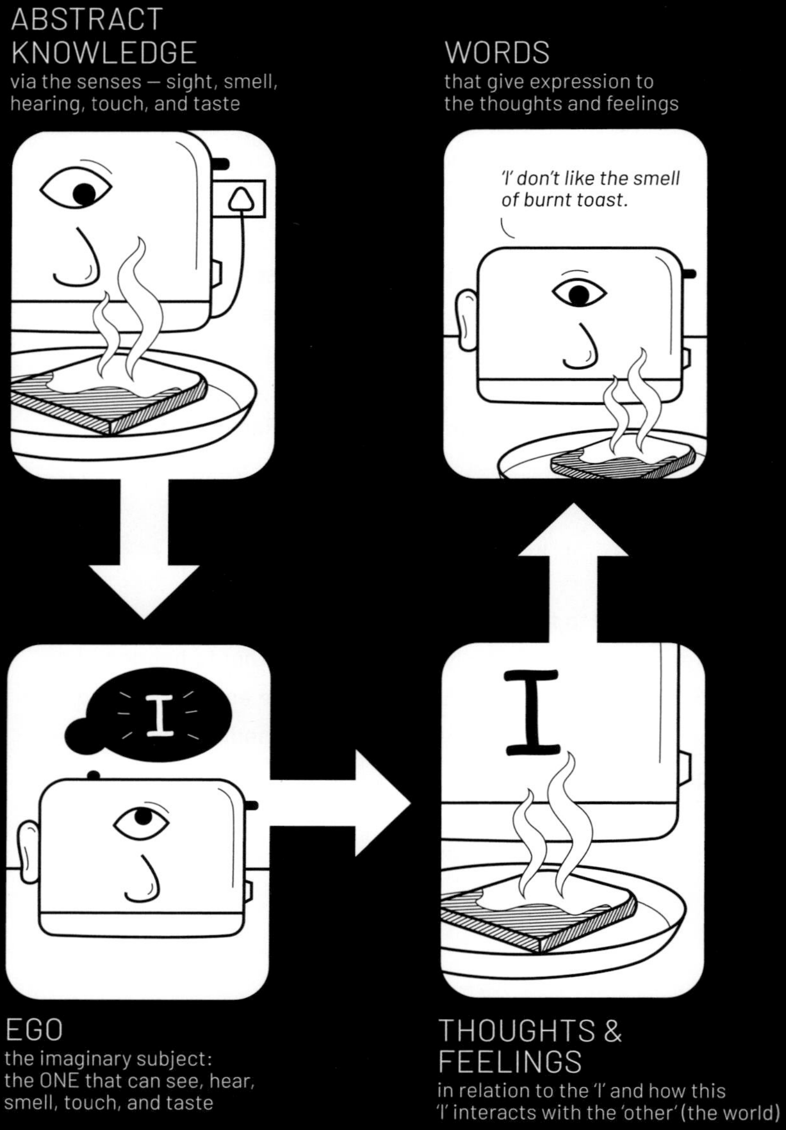
ABSTRACT KNOWLEDGE
via the senses — sight, smell, hearing, touch, and taste
WORDS
that give expression to the thoughts and feelings
'I' don't like the smell of burnt toast.
I
I
EGO
the imaginary subject: the ONE that can see, hear, smell, touch, and taste
THOUGHTS & FEELINGS
in relation to the 'I' and how this 'I' interacts with the 'other' (the world)

5.

TWINS SEPARATED
AT BIRTH

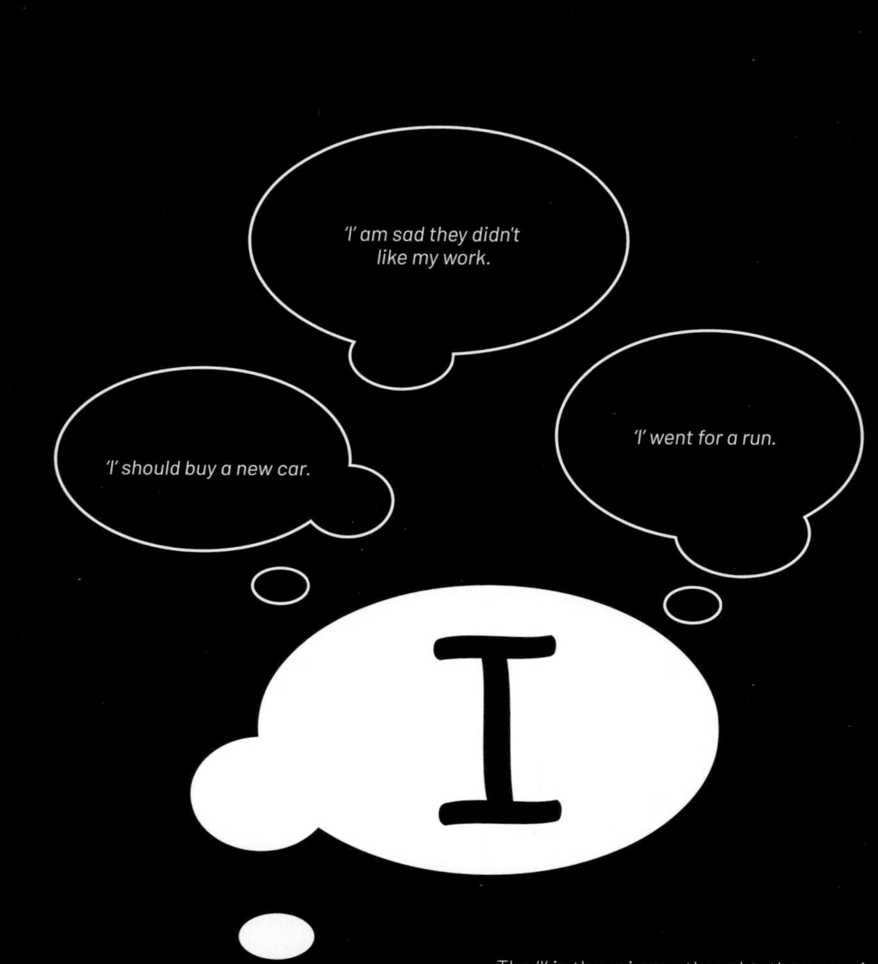

'I' am sad they didn't like my work.
'I' should buy a new car.
'I' went for a run.
I

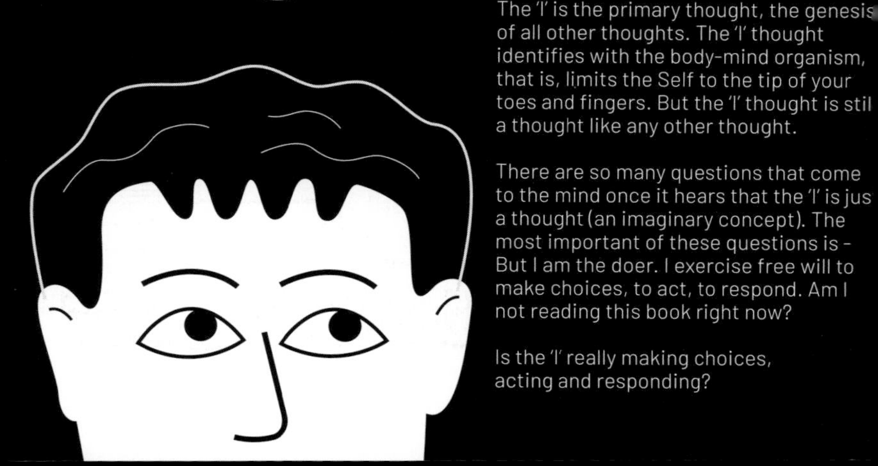

The 'I' is the primary thought, the genesis of all other thoughts. The 'I' thought identifies with the body-mind organism, that is, limits the Self to the tip of your toes and fingers. But the 'I' thought is stil a thought like any other thought.

There are so many questions that come to the mind once it hears that the 'I' is jus a thought (an imaginary concept). The most important of these questions is - But I am the doer. I exercise free will to make choices, to act, to respond. Am I not reading this book right now?

Is the 'I' really making choices, acting and responding?

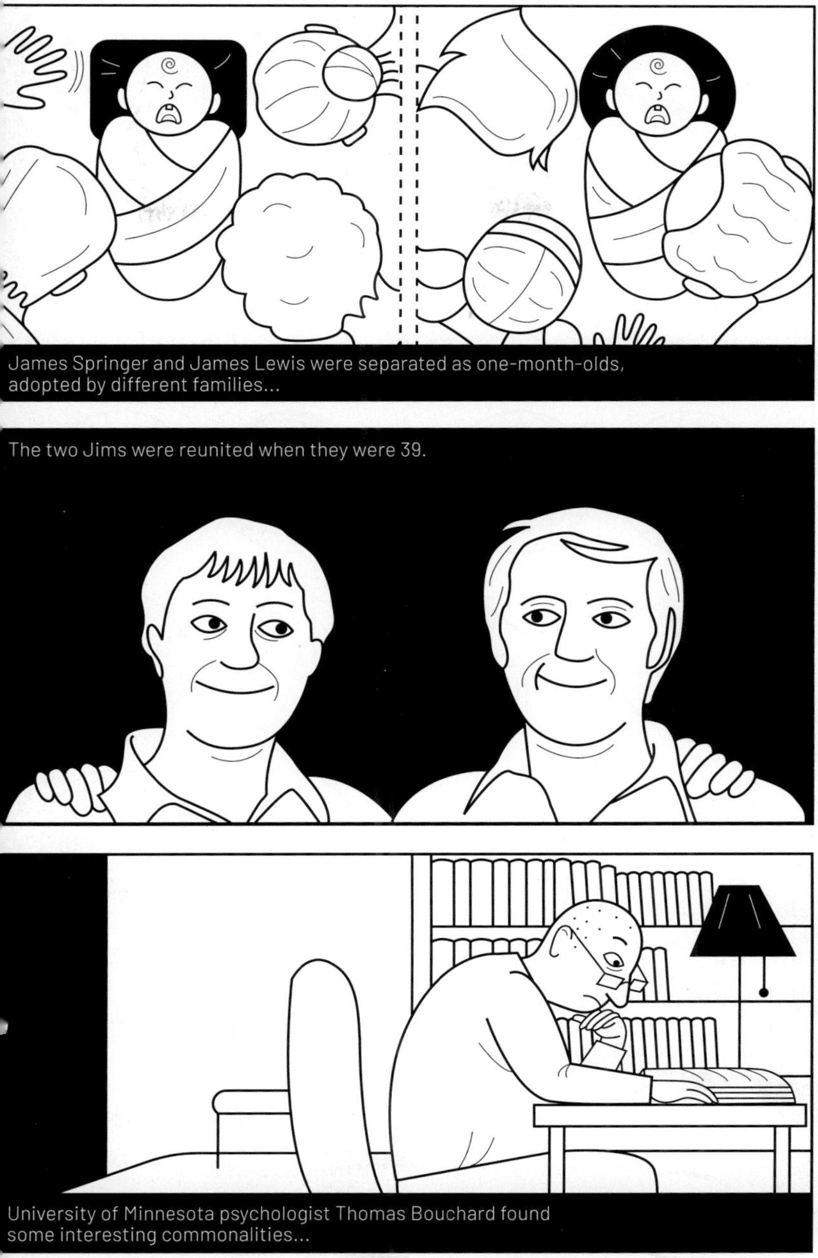
James Springer and James Lewis were separated as one-month-olds, adopted by different families...
The two Jims were reunited when they were 39.
University of Minnesota psychologist Thomas Bouchard found some interesting commonalities...

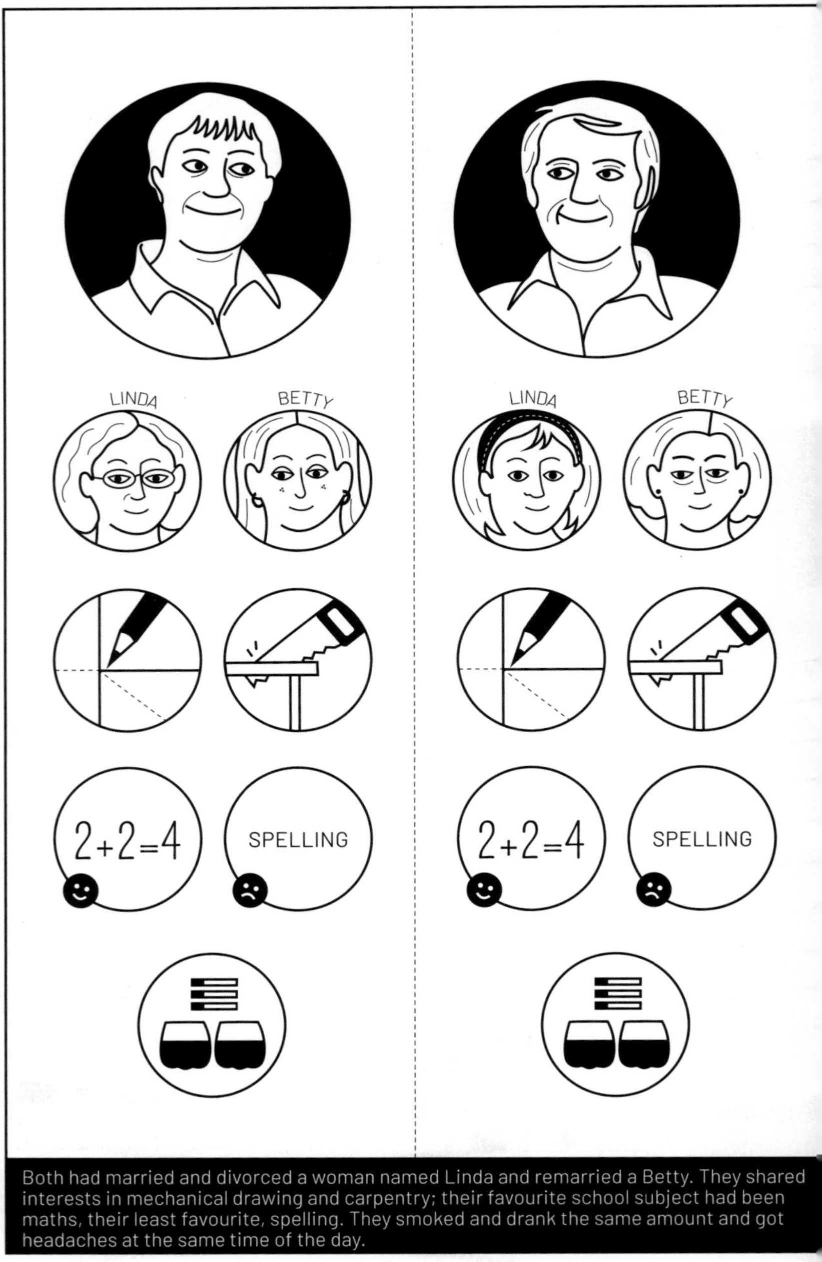
LINDA
BETTY
2+2=4
SPELLING
LINDA
BETTY
2+2=4
SPELLING

Both had married and divorced a woman named Linda and remarried a Betty. They shared interests in mechanical drawing and carpentry; their favourite school subject had been maths, their least favourite, spelling. They smoked and drank the same amount and got headaches at the same time of the day.

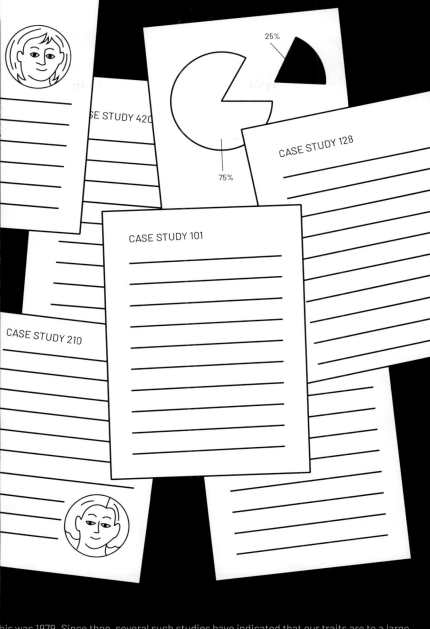

CASE STUDY 420

25%

75%

CASE STUDY 128

CASE STUDY 101

CASE STUDY 210

his was 1979. Since then, several such studies have indicated that our traits are to a large xtent inherited. So, how we respond to situations is heavily influenced by our genes. But nat's not all. It's also about the environment we grow up in.

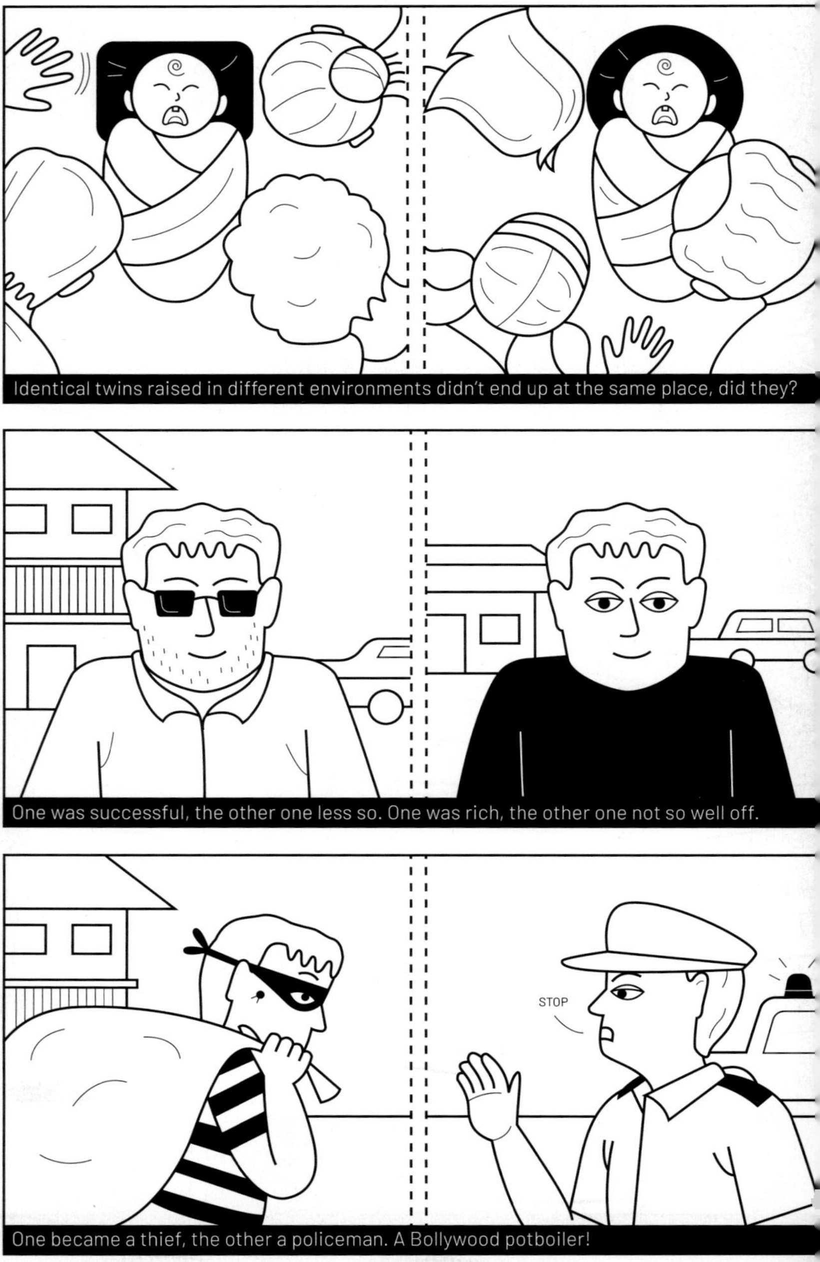
Identical twins raised in different environments didn't end up at the same place, did they?
One was successful, the other one less so. One was rich, the other one not so well off.
STOP
One became a thief, the other a policeman. A Bollywood potboiler!

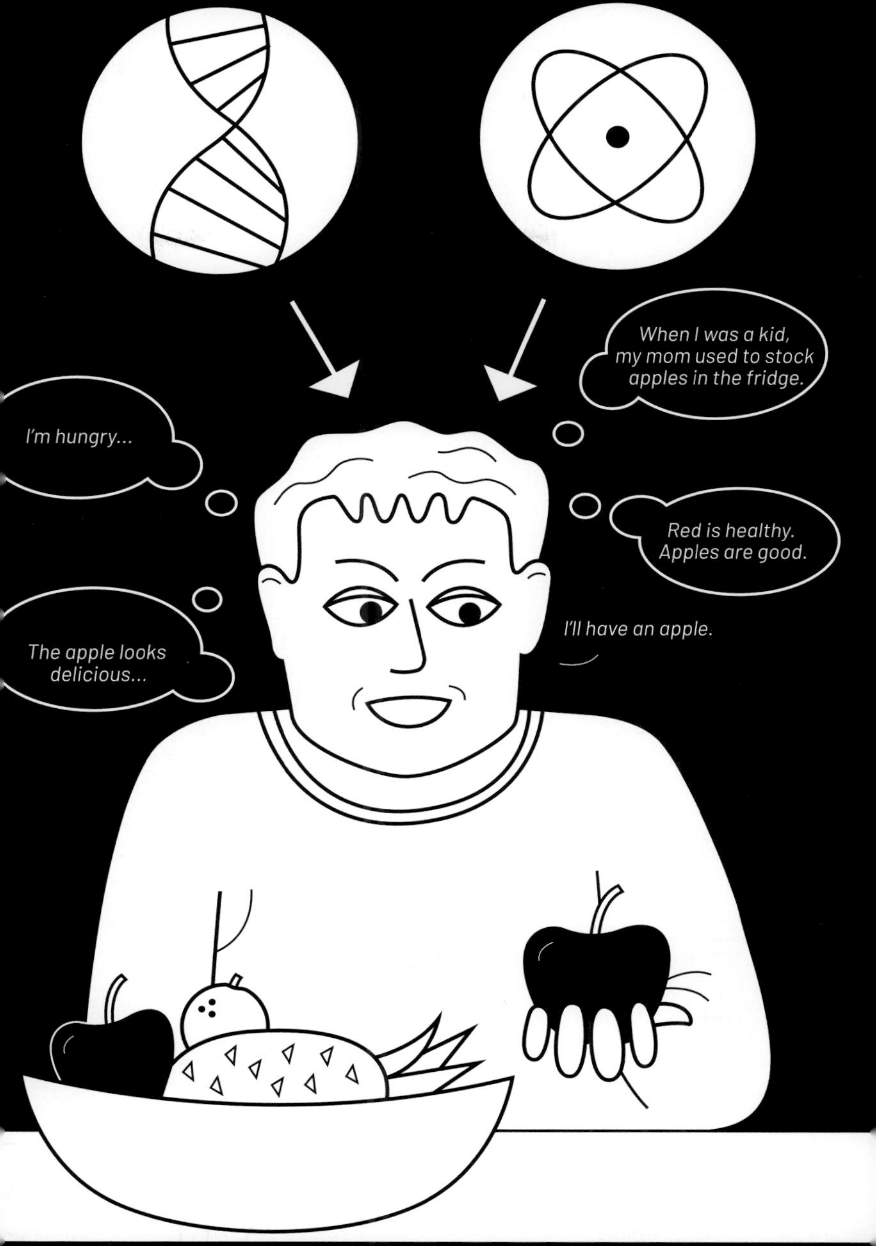

When I was a kid, my mom used to stock apples in the fridge.
I'm hungry...
Red is healthy. Apples are good.
I'll have an apple.
The apple looks delicious...

atest research into the role of genes and conditioning clearly affirms that everything we
o or sayor think or feel (all of it), is dictated by our genetic code and the environment that
e have grown up in(implying everything that's happened to us till the present).

But wait...

Which one of these things was in our control?

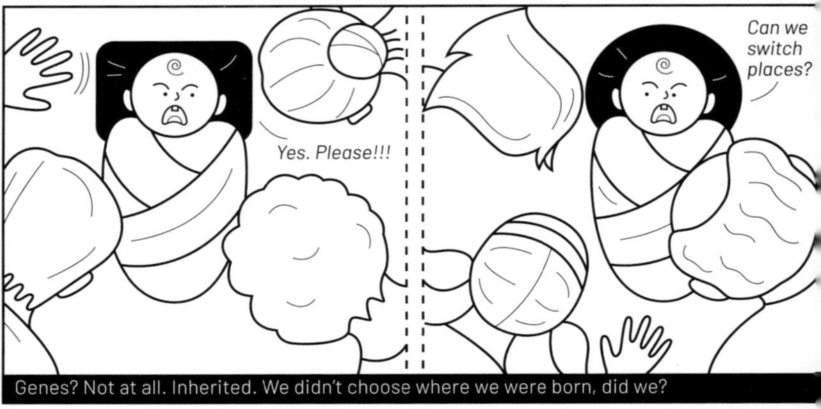
Yes. Please!!!
Can we switch places?
Genes? Not at all. Inherited. We didn't choose where we were born, did we?

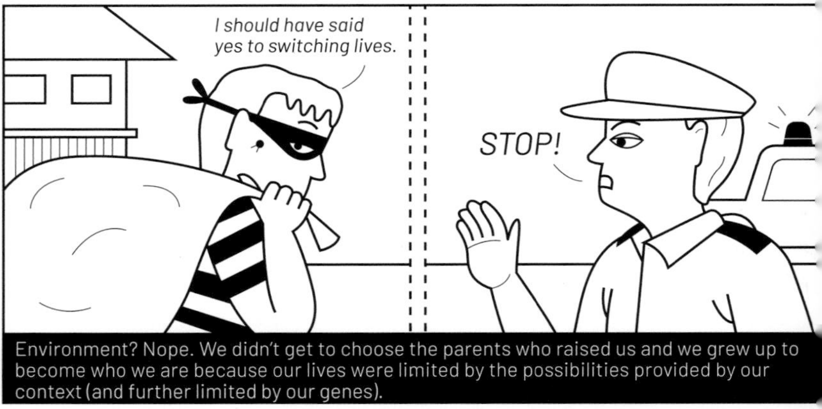
I should have said yes to switching lives.
STOP!
Environment? Nope. We didn't get to choose the parents who raised us and we grew up to become who we are because our lives were limited by the possibilities provided by our context (and further limited by our genes).

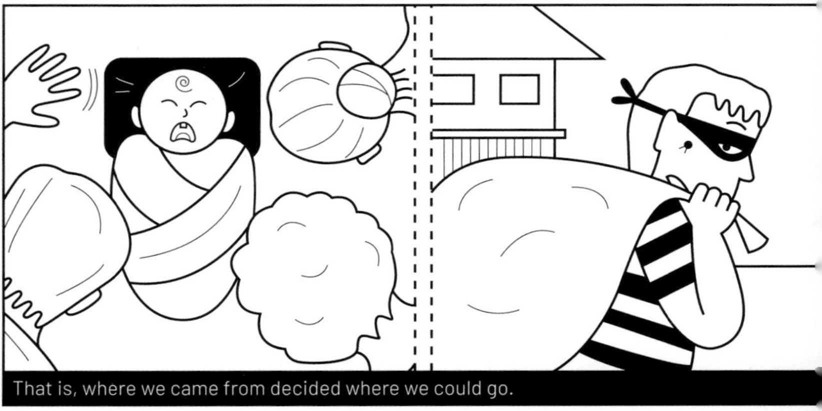
That is, where we came from decided where we could go.

There is nothing new about what's being said. The theory of genetics was first proposed a century and a half ago. Genes and conditioning and their relative influence have been hotly debated. However, recent research is clearly pointing to something that's even more radical.

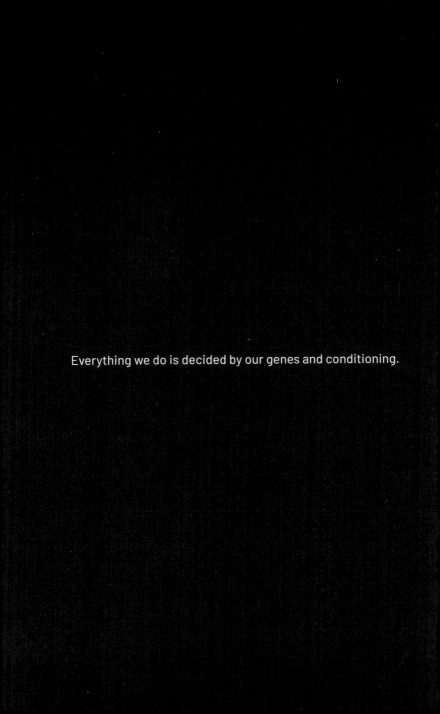

Everything we do is decided by our genes and conditioning.

We respond to external stimuli
but the response is pre-programmed, that is,
decided by our genes and conditioning.

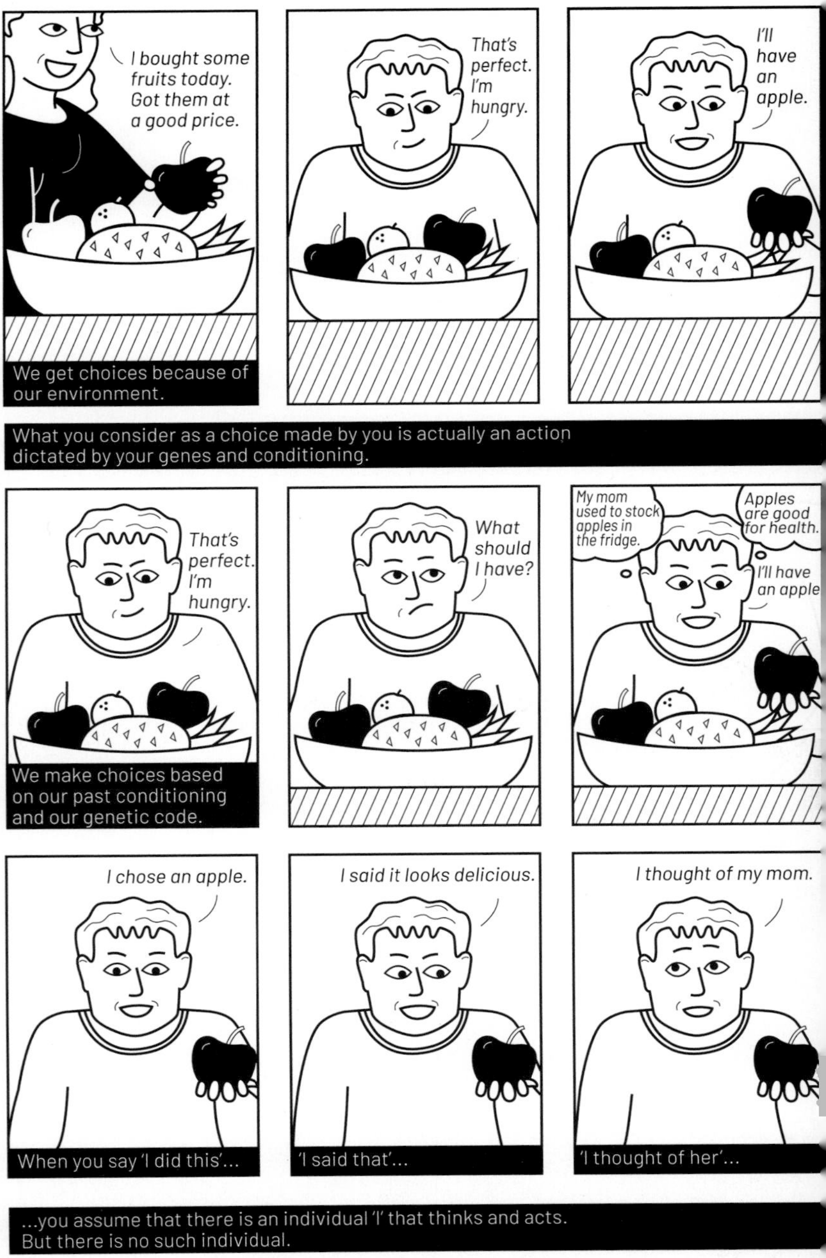
I bought some fruits today. Got them at a good price.
We get choices because of our environment.
That's perfect. I'm hungry.
I'll have an apple.
What you consider as a choice made by you is actually an action dictated by your genes and conditioning.
That's perfect. I'm hungry.
We make choices based on our past conditioning and our genetic code.
What should I have?
My mom used to stock apples in the fridge.
Apples are good for health.
I'll have an apple
I chose an apple.
When you say 'I did this'...
I said it looks delicious.
'I said that'...
I thought of my mom.
'I thought of her'...
...you assume that there is an individual 'I' that thinks and acts. But there is no such individual.

My mom used to stock apples in the fridge.
Apples are good for health.
I'll have an apple.
The body is a machine that thinks and acts in a particular way based on genes and conditioning.
Like a toaster that can only make toast...
the mind-body organism has to do what it has to do.

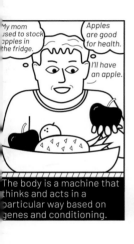

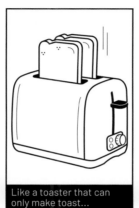

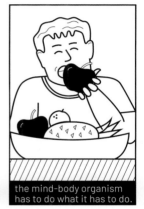

Do you have any control over the next thought that pops up in your head?

6.

THE GRAND ILLUSION

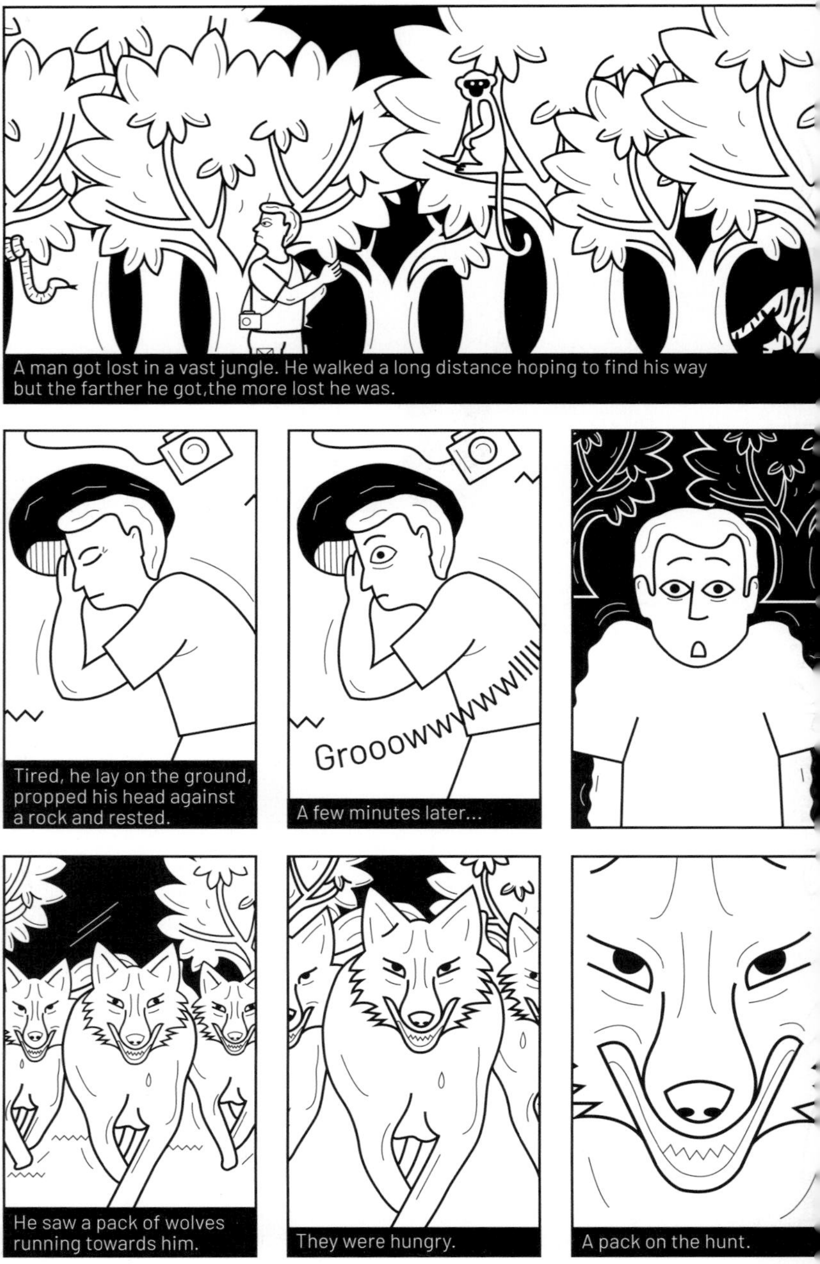
A man got lost in a vast jungle. He walked a long distance hoping to find his way but the farther he got,the more lost he was.
Tired, he lay on the ground, propped his head against a rock and rested.
Grooowwwwwwllll
A few minutes later...
He saw a pack of wolves running towards him.
They were hungry.
A pack on the hunt.

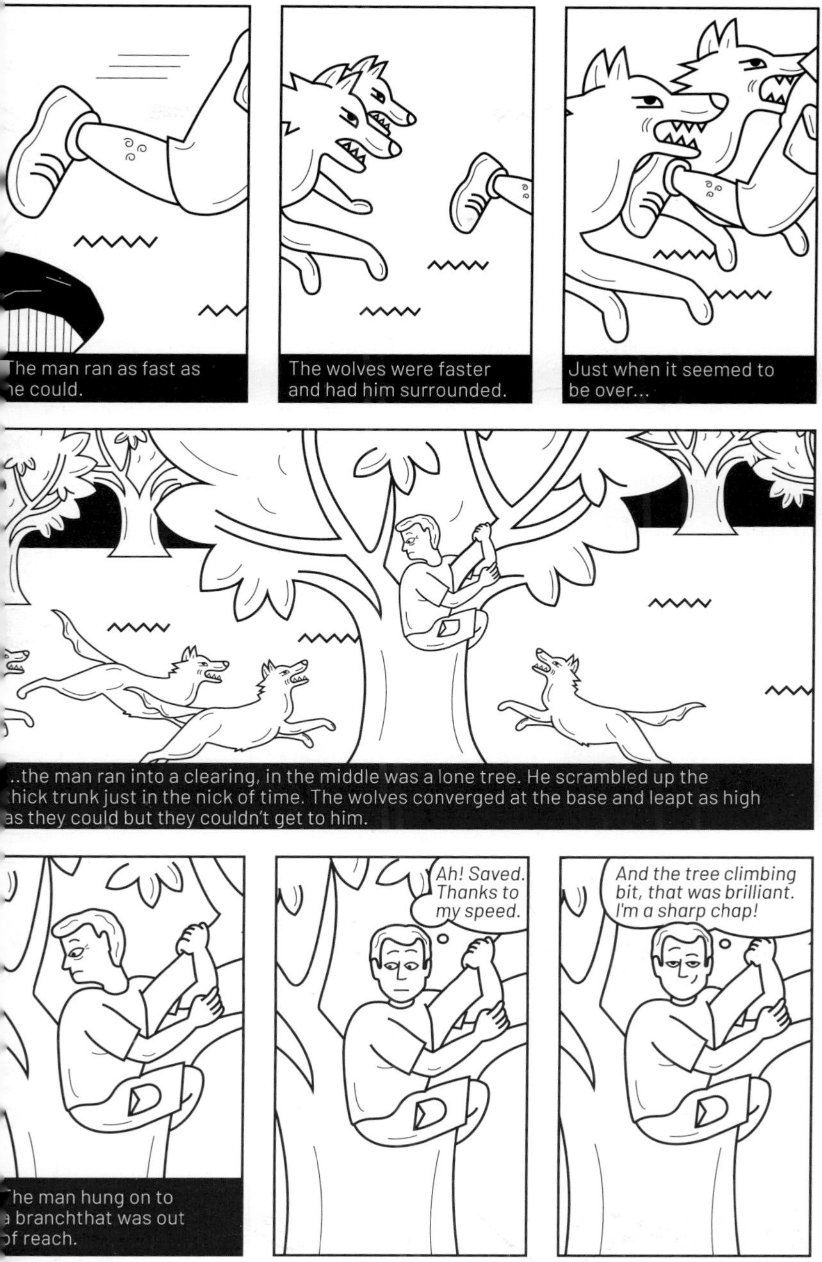
The man ran as fast as
he could.
The wolves were faster
and had him surrounded.
Just when it seemed to
be over...
..the man ran into a clearing, in the middle was a lone tree. He scrambled up the
thick trunk just in the nick of time. The wolves converged at the base and leapt as high
as they could but they couldn't get to him.
The man hung on to
a branchthat was out
of reach.
Ah! Saved. Thanks to my speed.
And the tree climbing bit, that was brilliant. I'm a sharp chap!

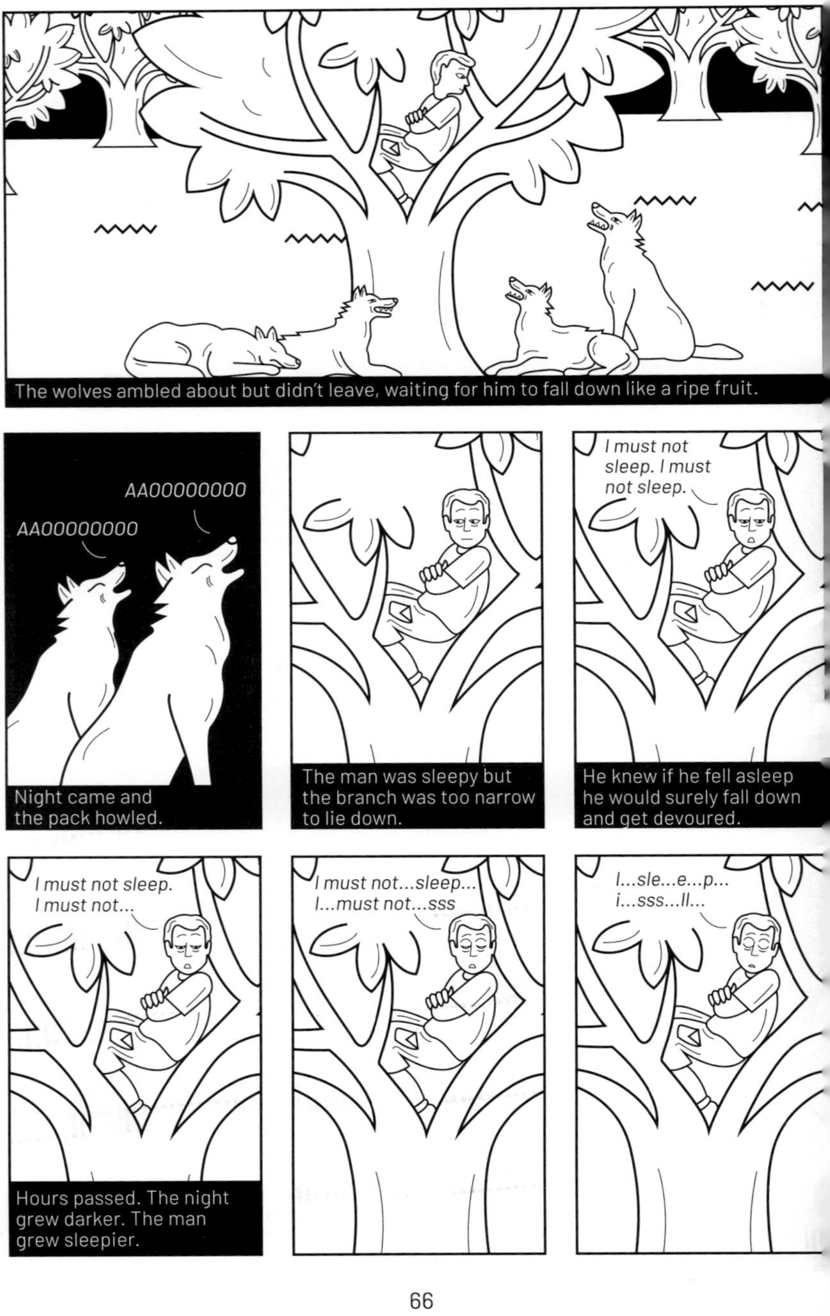

The wolves ambled about but didn't leave, waiting for him to fall down like a ripe fruit.
AAOOOOOOOO
AAOOOOOOOO
Night came and the pack howled.
The man was sleepy but the branch was too narrow to lie down.
I must not sleep. I must not sleep.
He knew if he fell asleep he would surely fall down and get devoured.
I must not sleep. I must not...
Hours passed. The night grew darker. The man grew sleepier.
I must not...sleep... I...must not...sss
I...sle...e...p... i...sss...ll...

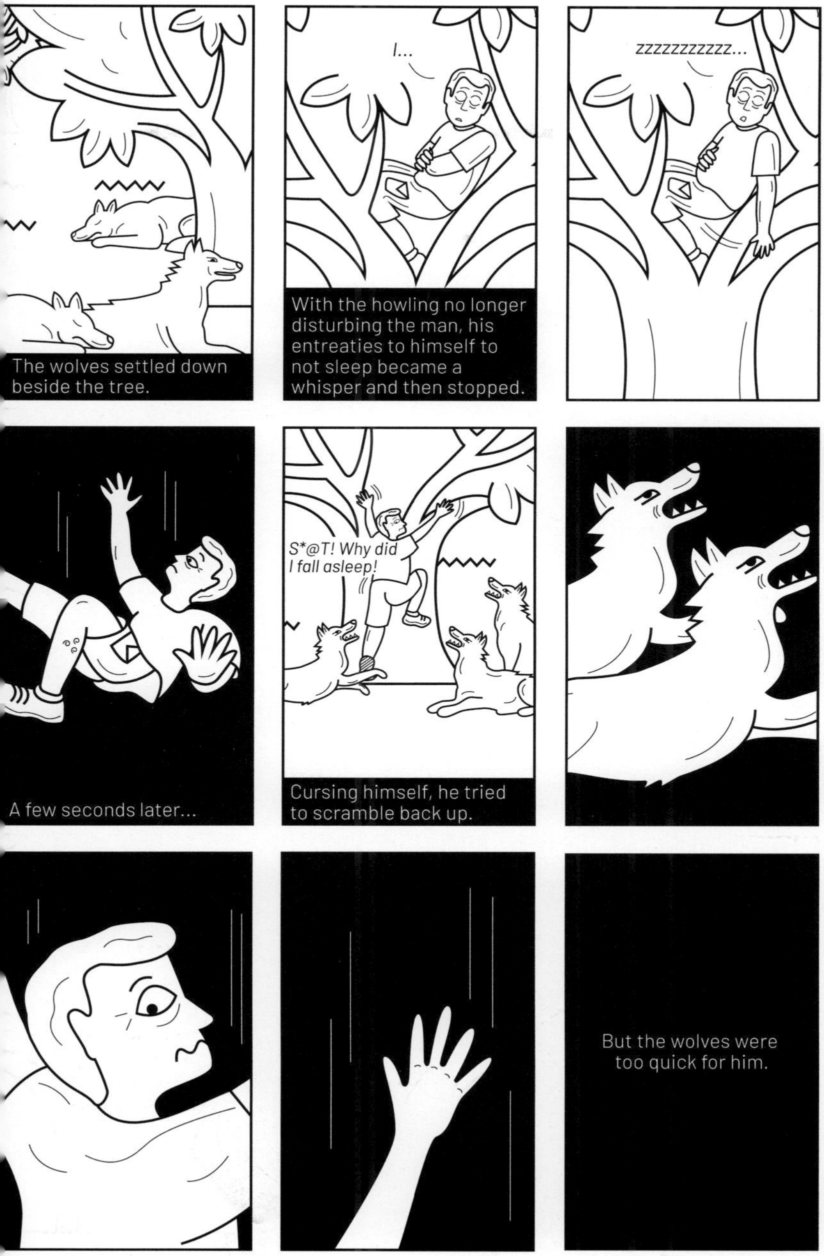

The wolves settled down beside the tree.
I...
With the howling no longer disturbing the man, his entreaties to himself to not sleep became a whisper and then stopped.
ZZZZZZZZZZZ...
A few seconds later...
S*@T! Why did I fall asleep!
Cursing himself, he tried to scramble back up.
But the wolves were too quick for him.

The man congratulates himself (his 'I') for running fast and climbing up the tree. He tells himself (his 'I' telling itself) not to fall asleep.

Like most of us, the man hasn't realized that the 'I' doesn't control thoughts and actions.

He ran because his mind-body was programmed to respond this way, he climbed up for the same reason, and he, finally, couldn't keep himself awake because he wasn't programmed to do that.

But in this story, the man's ego sense 'I' takes the credit, gets blamed — having done nothing, isn't that something?

This is the GRAND ILLUSION.

7.

WORKING MIND/THINKING MIND

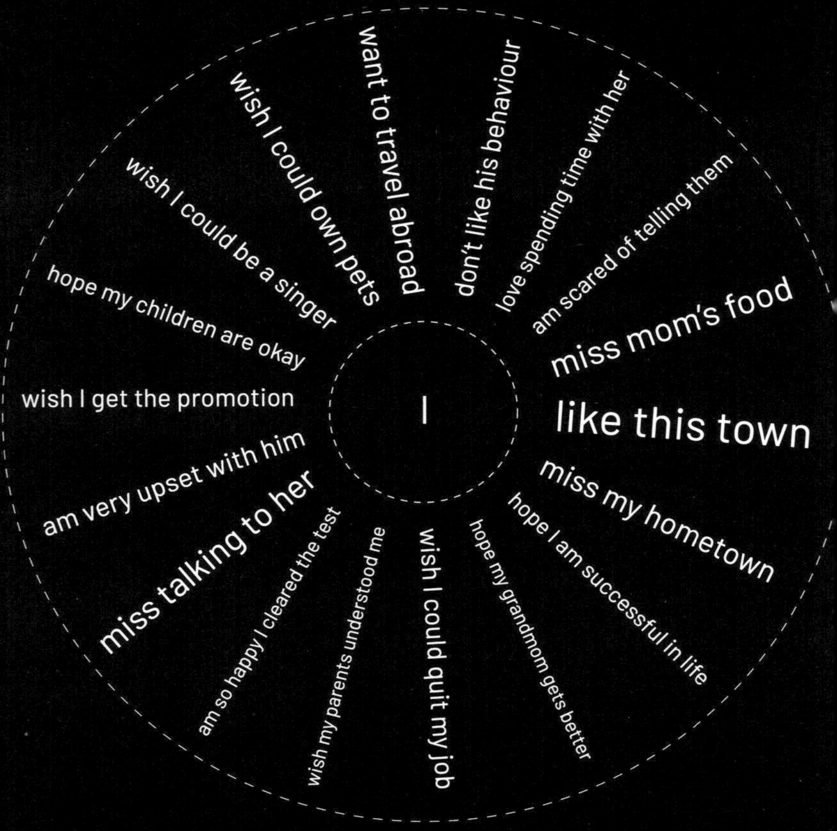
I
want to travel abroad
don't like his behaviour
love spending time with her
am scared of telling them
miss mom's food
like this town
miss my hometown
hope I am successful in life
hope my grandmom gets better
wish I could quit my job
wish my parents understood me
am so happy I cleared the test
miss talking to her
am very upset with him
wish I get the promotion
hope my children are okay
wish I could be a singer
wish I could own pets

Have you noticed the tremendous, painful weight of the 'I'?

I have to do this or else I'll be in a soup...
If only I hadn't done that...
I can't do that and he can...
She made me suffer...
He will definitely do something to harm my reputation...

It goes on and on. The regret and anxiety related to what was done to you or by you in the past or what you have to do or someone else will do to you in the future — isn't that a significant part of our mental narrative?

But if 'I' is not the doer, then what's the point of worrying about what you did or will do? Why be anxious about what will happen in the future and regret what you did in the past? Why not live from moment to moment, being fully attentive to the present?

AN INTERPRETATION OF THE ZEN KOAN: 'THE FIRST PRINCIPLE'

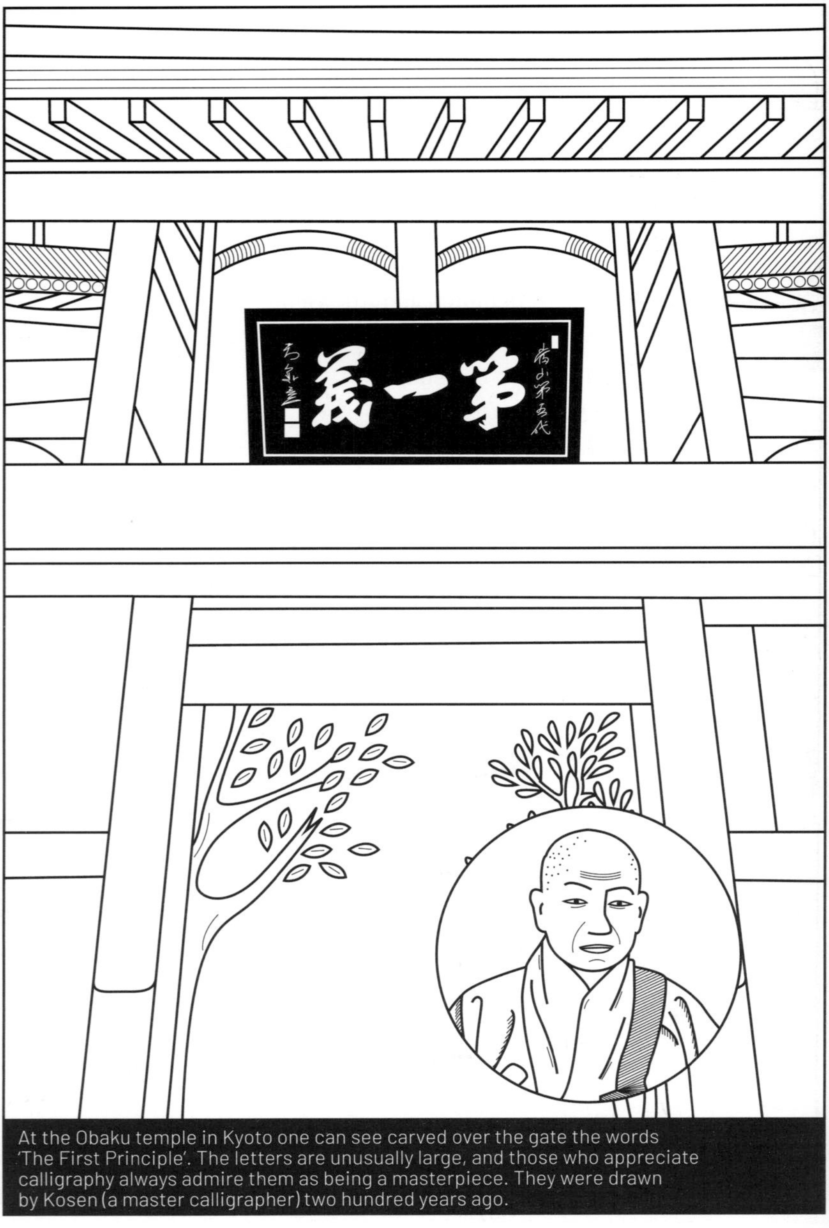
第一義

At the Obaku temple in Kyoto one can see carved over the gate the words 'The First Principle'. The letters are unusually large, and those who appreciate calligraphy always admire them as being a masterpiece. They were drawn by Kosen (a master calligrapher) two hundred years ago.

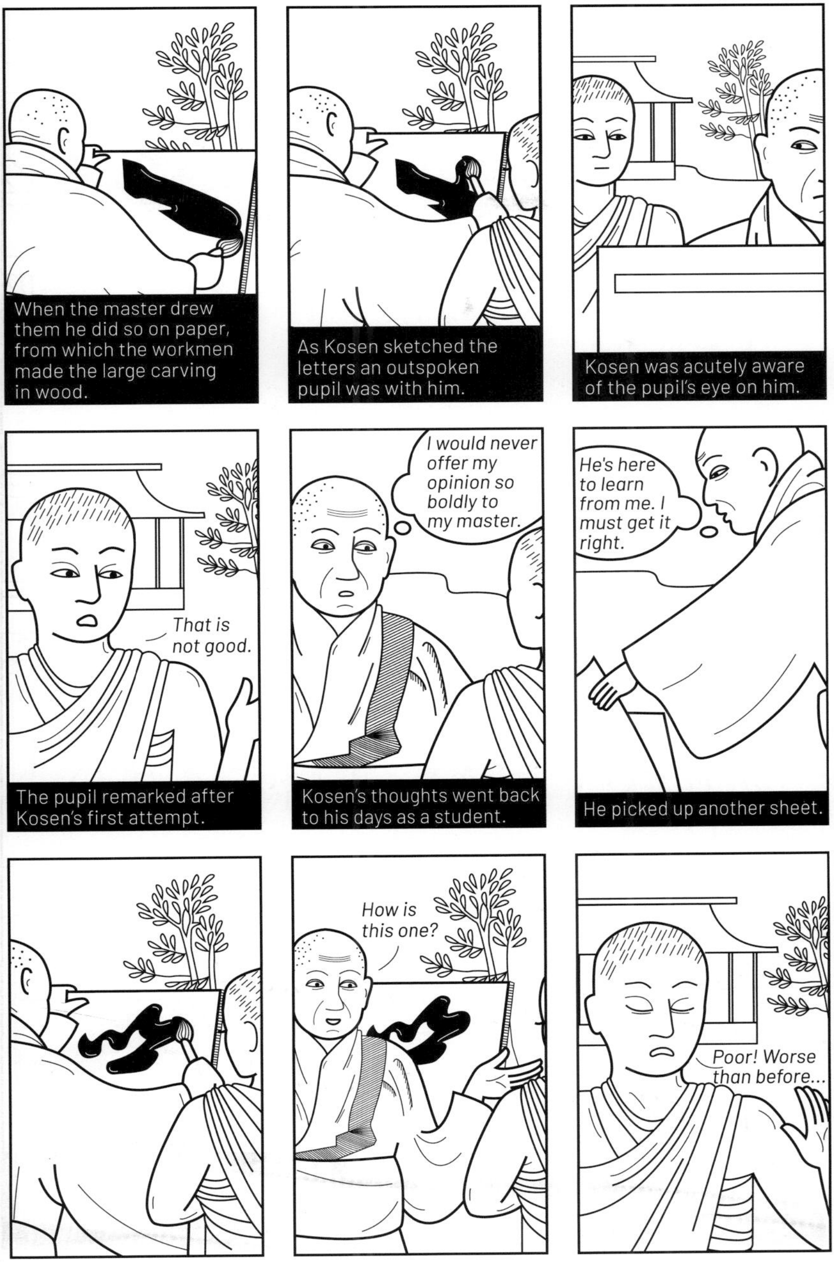
When the master drew them he did so on paper, from which the workmen made the large carving in wood.
As Kosen sketched the letters an outspoken pupil was with him.
Kosen was acutely aware of the pupil's eye on him.
That is not good.
The pupil remarked after Kosen's first attempt.
I would never offer my opinion so boldly to my master.
Kosen's thoughts went back to his days as a student.
He's here to learn from me. I must get it right.
He picked up another sheet.
How is this one?
Poor! Worse than before...

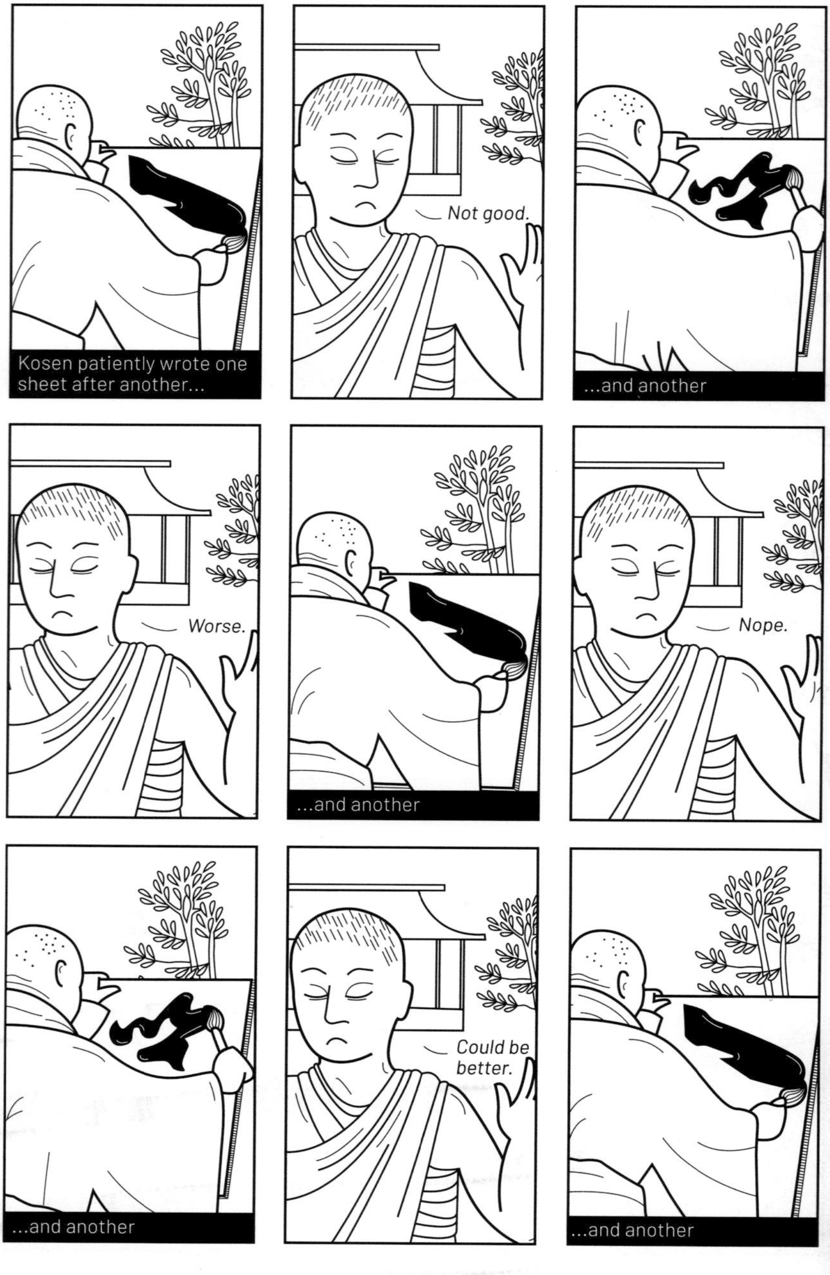

Kosen patiently wrote one sheet after another...
Not good.
...and another
Worse.
...and another
Nope.
...and another
Could be better.
...and another

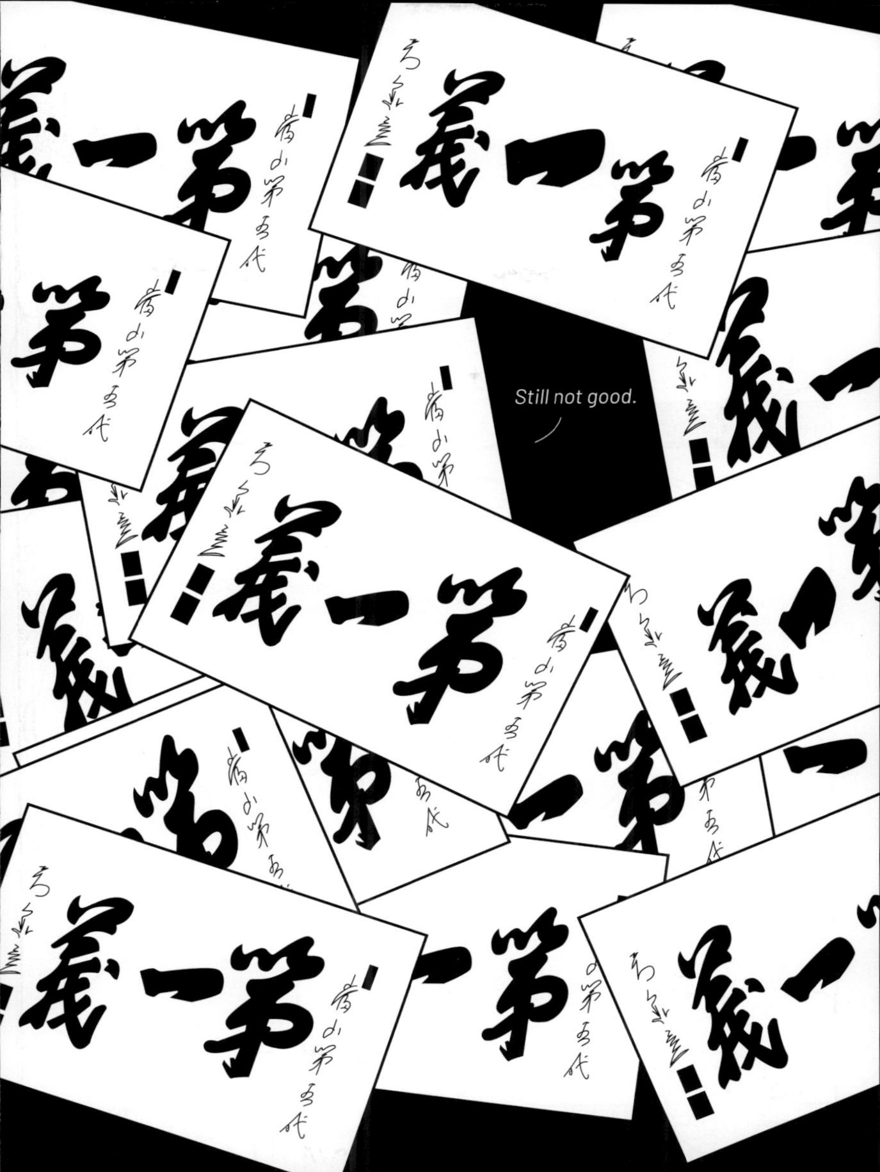
Still not good.

...until eighty-four First Principles had accumulated, still without the approval of the pupil.

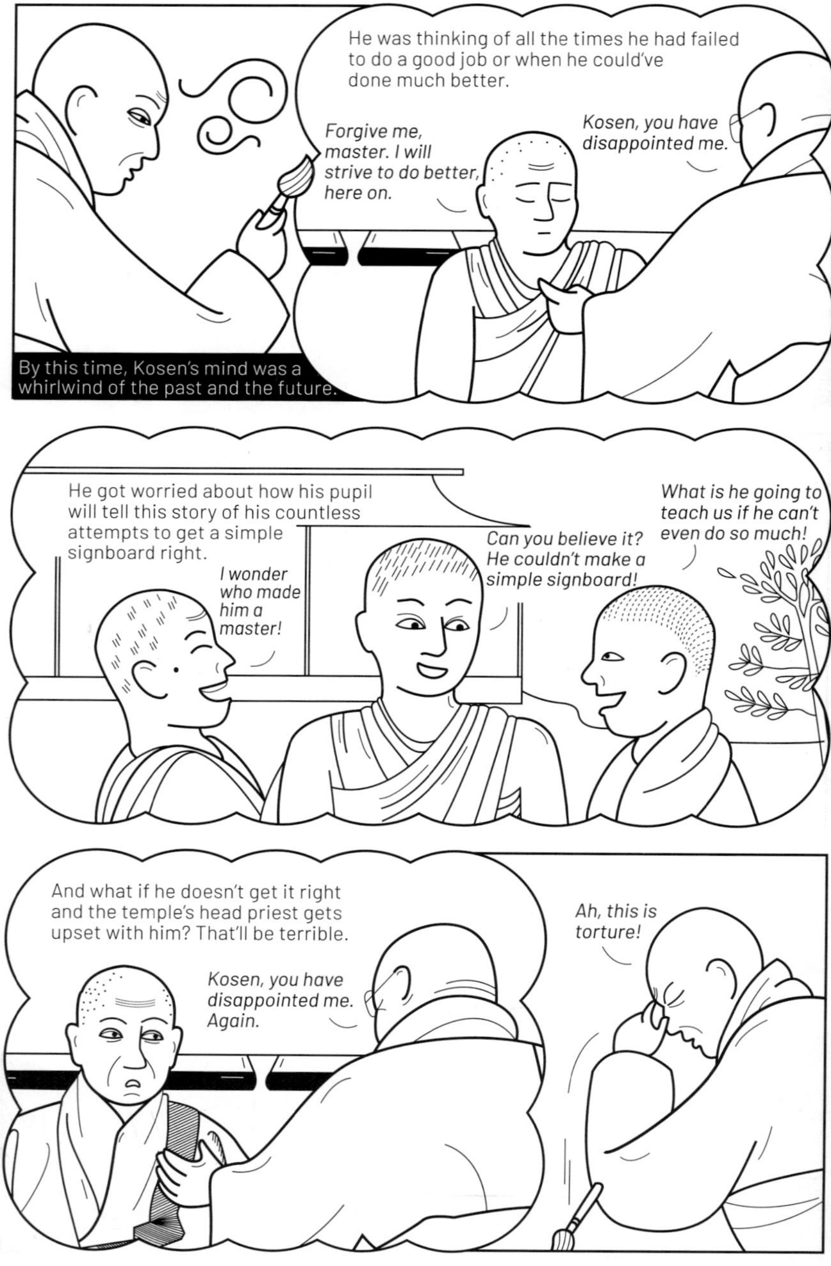
By this time, Kosen's mind was a whirlwind of the past and the future.
He was thinking of all the times he had failed to do a good job or when he could've done much better.
Kosen, you have disappointed me.
Forgive me, master. I will strive to do better, here on.
He got worried about how his pupil will tell this story of his countless attempts to get a simple signboard right.
I wonder who made him a master!
Can you believe it? He couldn't make a simple signboard!
What is he going to teach us if he can't even do so much!
And what if he doesn't get it right and the temple's head priest gets upset with him? That'll be terrible.
Kosen, you have disappointed me. Again.
Ah, this is torture!

The young pupil stepped out to run a quick errand.

Now this is my chance to escape his keen eye!

Kosen wrote hurriedly with a mind free from distraction.

The First Principle

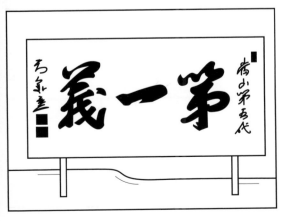

Masterpiece!!

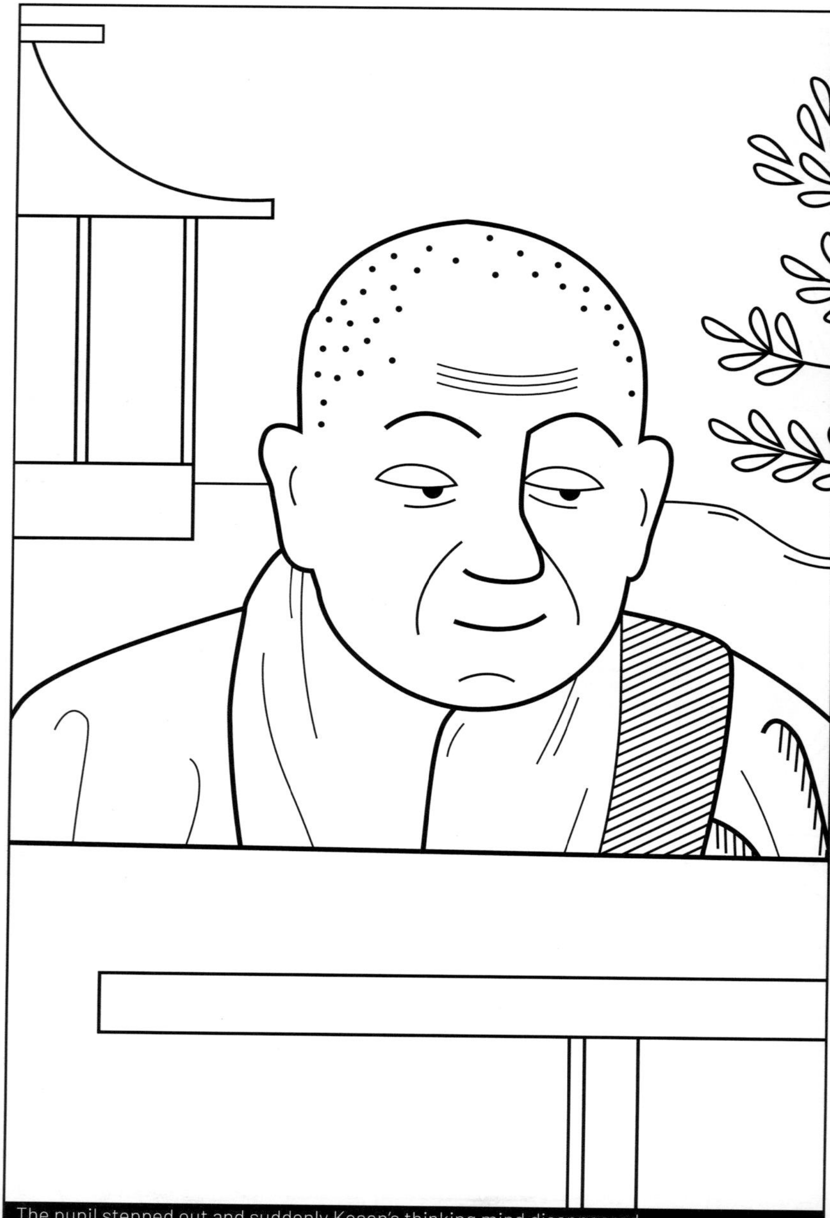

The pupil stepped out and suddenly Kosen's thinking mind disappeared, and the working mind took over (the mind in the moment).

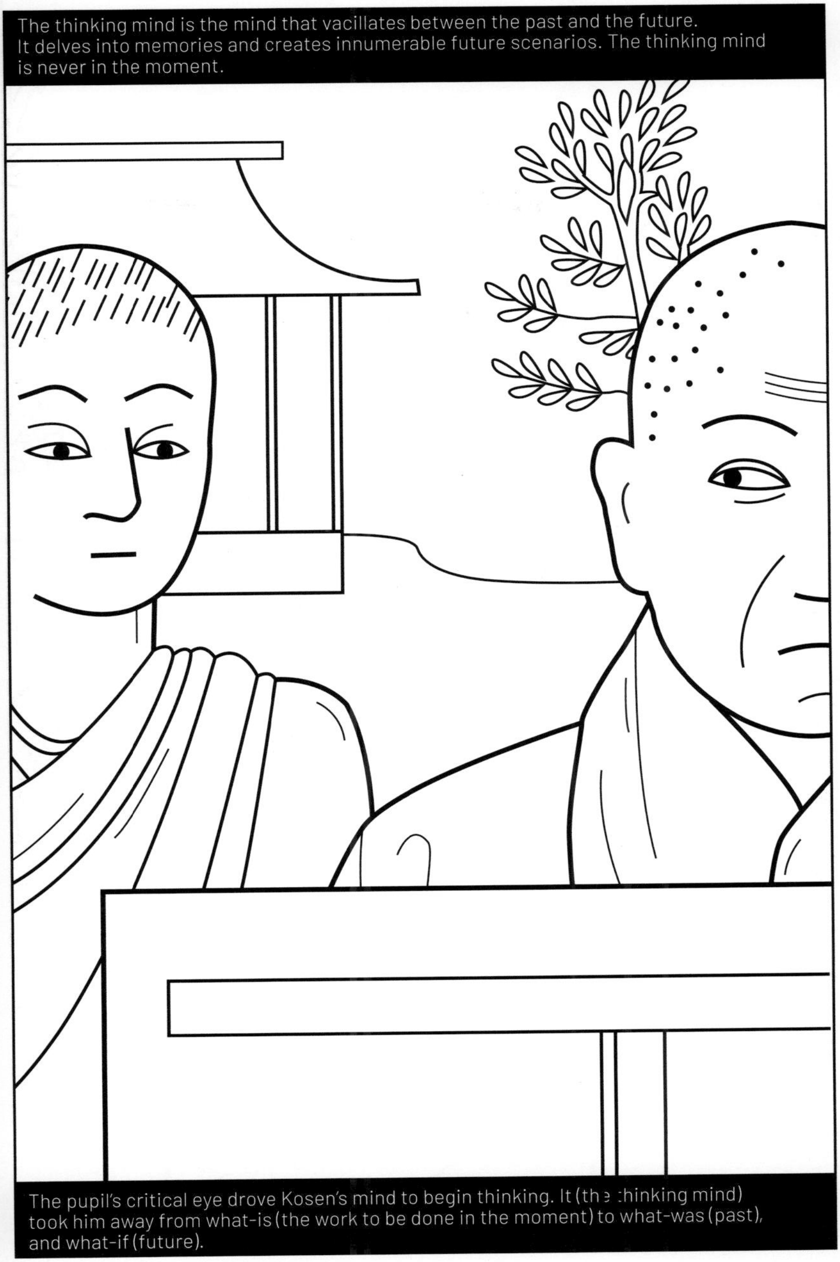
The thinking mind is the mind that vacillates between the past and the future. It delves into memories and creates innumerable future scenarios. The thinking mind is never in the moment.
The pupil's critical eye drove Kosen's mind to begin thinking. It (the thinking mind) took him away from what-is (the work to be done in the moment) to what-was (past), and what-if (future).

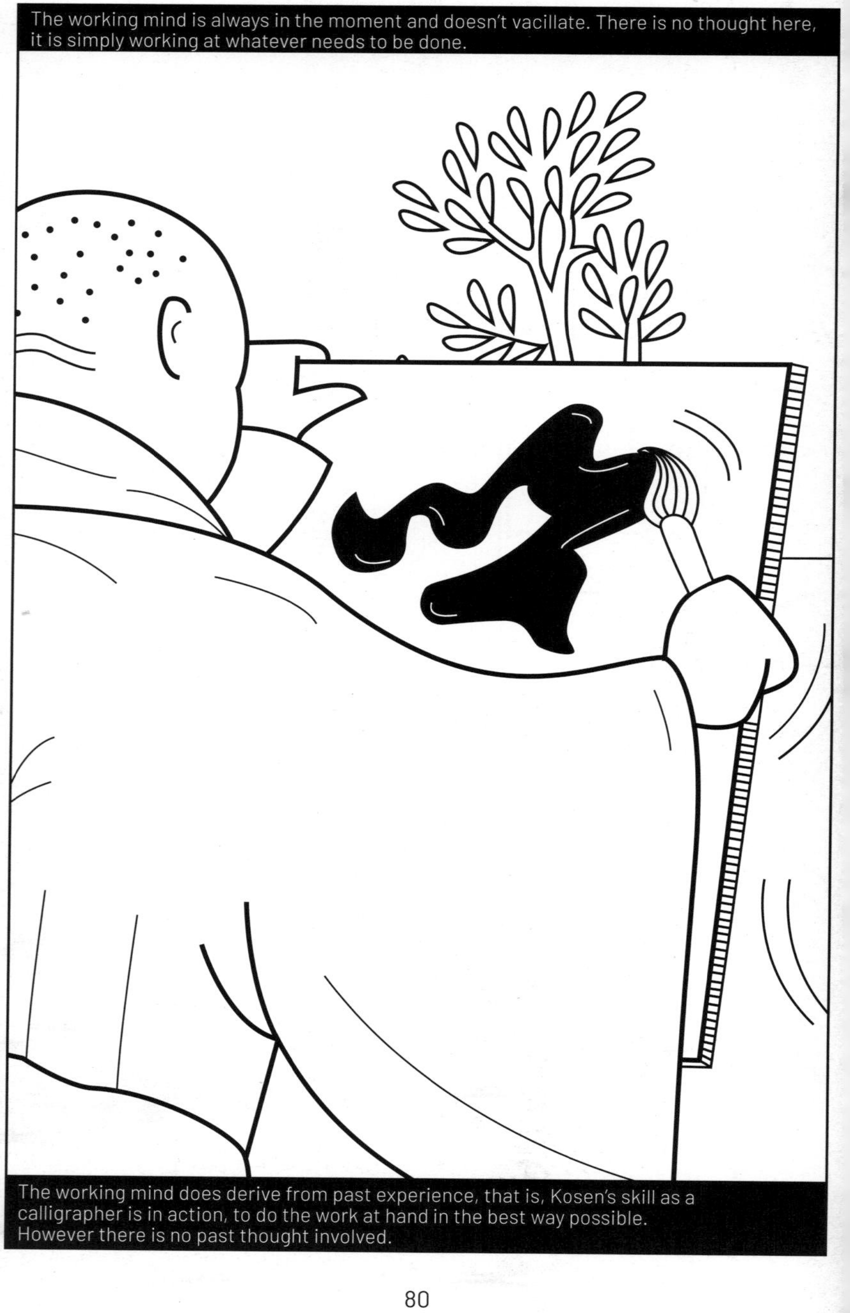
The working mind is always in the moment and doesn't vacillate. There is no thought here, it is simply working at whatever needs to be done.
The working mind does derive from past experience, that is, Kosen's skill as a calligrapher is in action, to do the work at hand in the best way possible. However there is no past thought involved.

Quietening the thinking mind and letting the working mind do what needs to be done is the gateway to peace and happiness.

So how does one cultivate the working mind?

By knowing that one is not the doer.

Abandoning doership will immediately quieten the thinking mind.

In this example, if Kosen had the realization (a complete acceptance) that he is not the doer then the past and the future thoughts wouldn't have appeared in his mind. Because 'I did' something in the past, therefore, a regret because 'I will fail to do something' in the future and hence a worry.

But if I'm not the doer then who is failing and who has regrets?

In the absence of a doer, worrying what 'I'll' do and 'I' won't be able to do is of no consequence. Worries are pointless. Think about it.

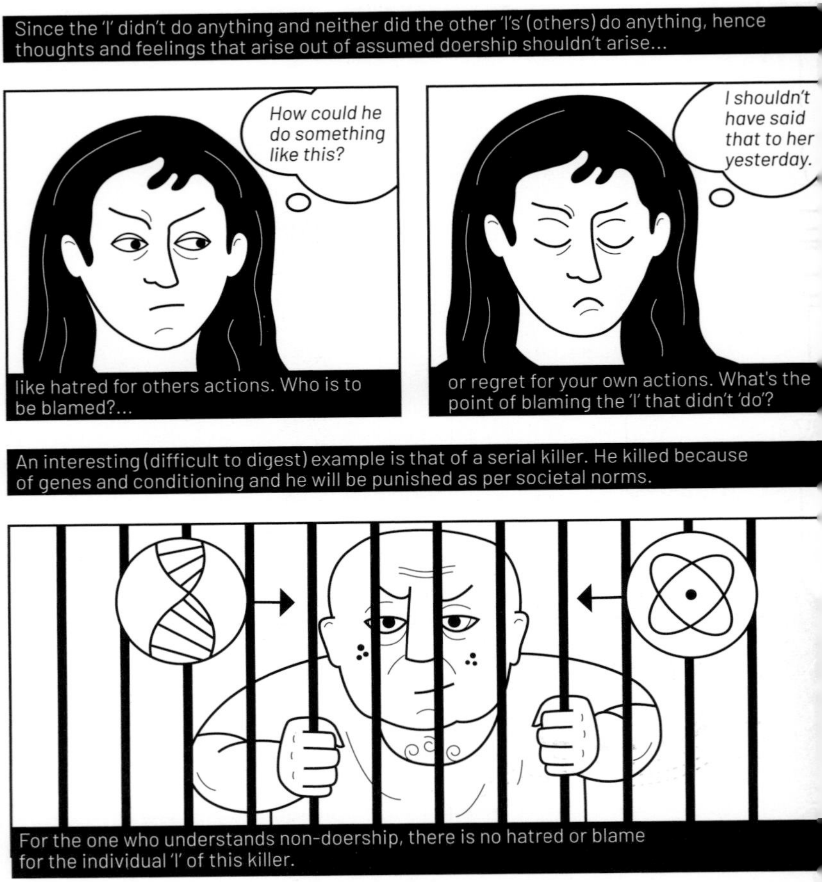
Since the 'I' didn't do anything and neither did the other 'I's' (others) do anything, hence thoughts and feelings that arise out of assumed doership shouldn't arise...
How could he do something like this?
like hatred for others actions. Who is to be blamed?...
I shouldn't have said that to her yesterday.
or regret for your own actions. What's the point of blaming the 'I' that didn't 'do'?
An interesting (difficult to digest) example is that of a serial killer. He killed because of genes and conditioning and he will be punished as per societal norms.
For the one who understands non-doership, there is no hatred or blame for the individual 'I' of this killer.

Sri Ramana Maharshi sums it up when he says:

'Actions form no bondage. Bondage is only the false notion. "I am the doer." Leave off such thoughts and let the body and senses play their role, unimpeded by your interference.'

Whatever needs to be done, your body-mind organism will do and what's going to happen will happen. As Krishna told Arjuna in the Bhagavad Gita,

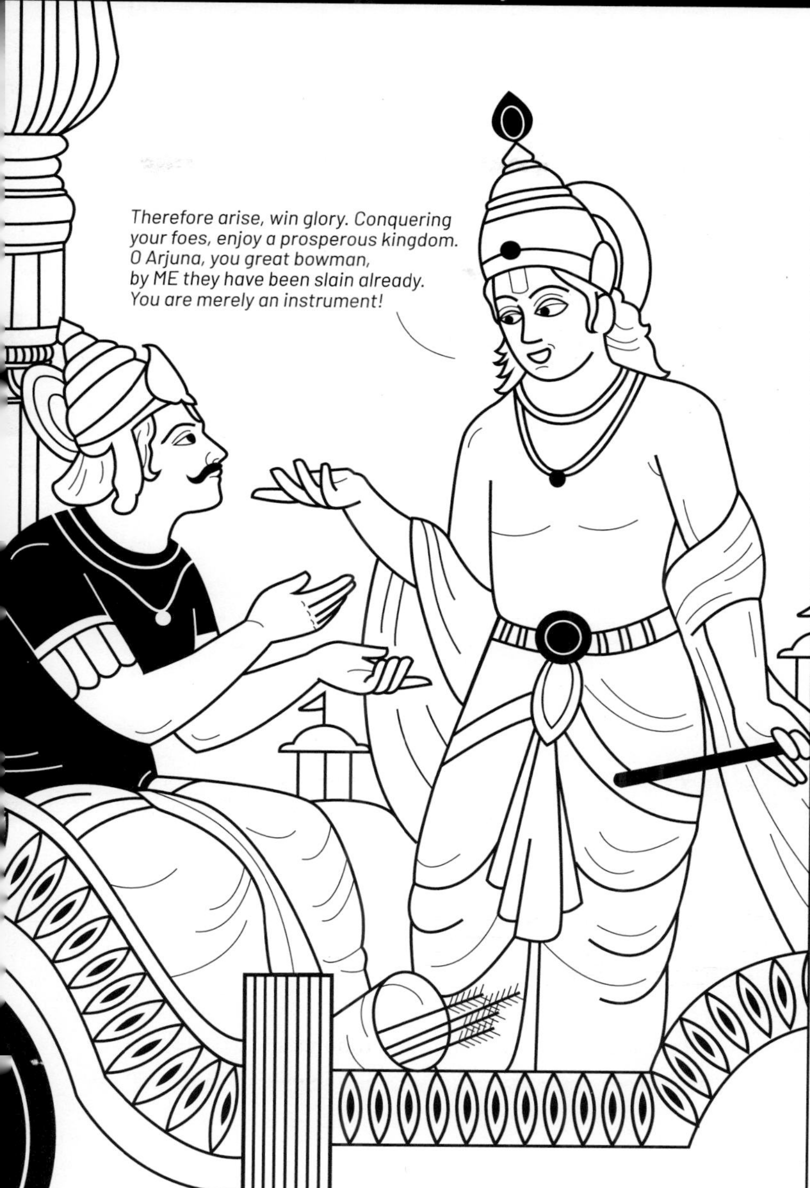
Therefore arise, win glory. Conquering your foes, enjoy a prosperous kingdom. O Arjuna, you great bowman, by ME they have been slain already. You are merely an instrument!

Notice that Krishna tells him to act (to conquer his foes) and also that they are slain already by HIM. These two concepts can coexist as beautifully explained in the Bhagavad Gita:

No man can, even for a moment, rest without
doing work; for everyone is caused to act in spite of himself,
by the 'gunas of nature'.*

~The Bhagavad Gita (Ch 3, Verse 5/43)

∞

He whose nature is deluded by egoism, thinks 'I am the doer'.

~The Bhagavad Gita (Ch 3, Verse 27/43)

*read genes and conditioning

Some folks, on reading this wonder

If I am not the doer then why don't I just lie on the bed all day long and do nothing?

or

If I am not the doer then why don't I go out and murder someone?

Both the questions are flawed. You can't lie down all day long till it's in your genes and conditioning to do that. You can't murder someone till it's in your genes and conditioning to do that.

There is 'no doer' doesn't imply that your body won't be the instrument of action. It will act according to its genes and conditioning.

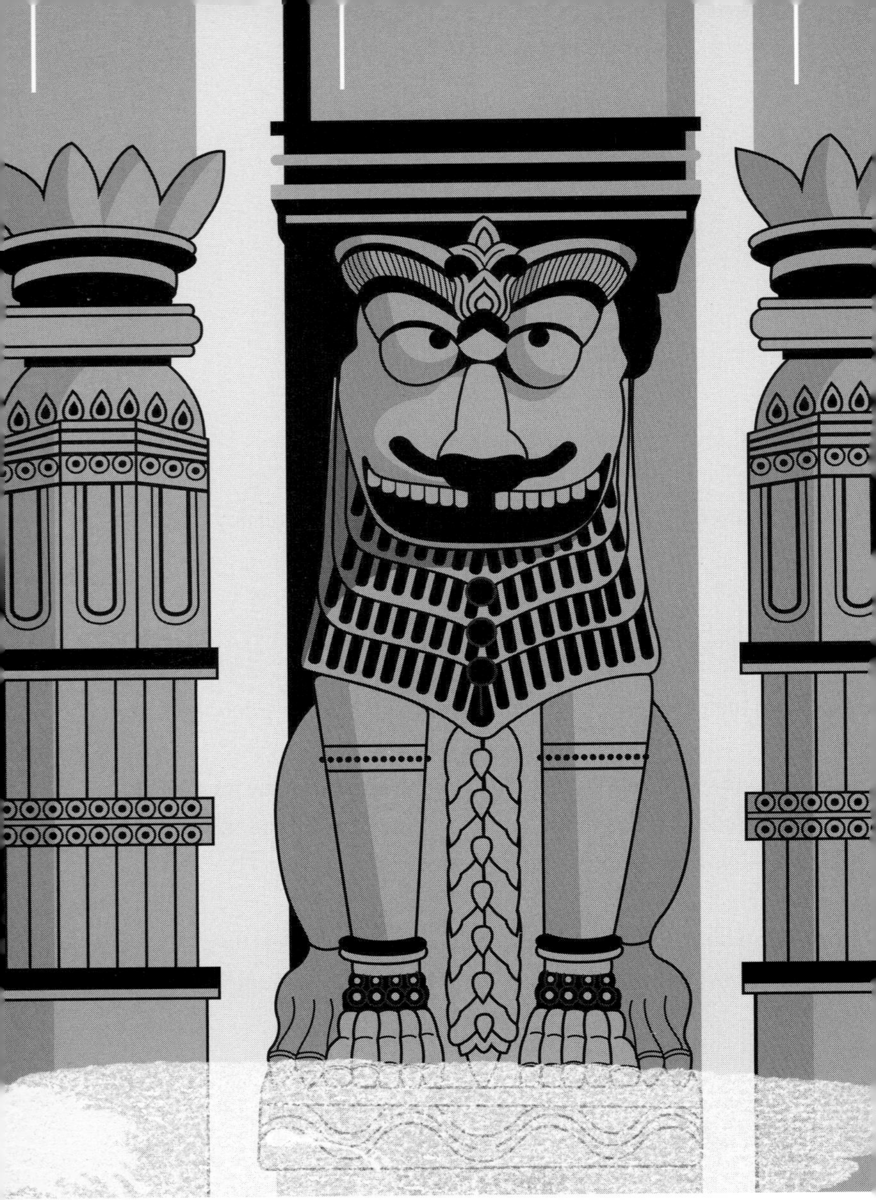

The Lord bears the burden of the world. Know that the spurious ego which presumes to bear that burden is like a sculptured figure at the foc of a temple tower which appears to sustain the tower's weight.

~ Ramana Maharshi

PART 2

THE LEAP OF FAITH

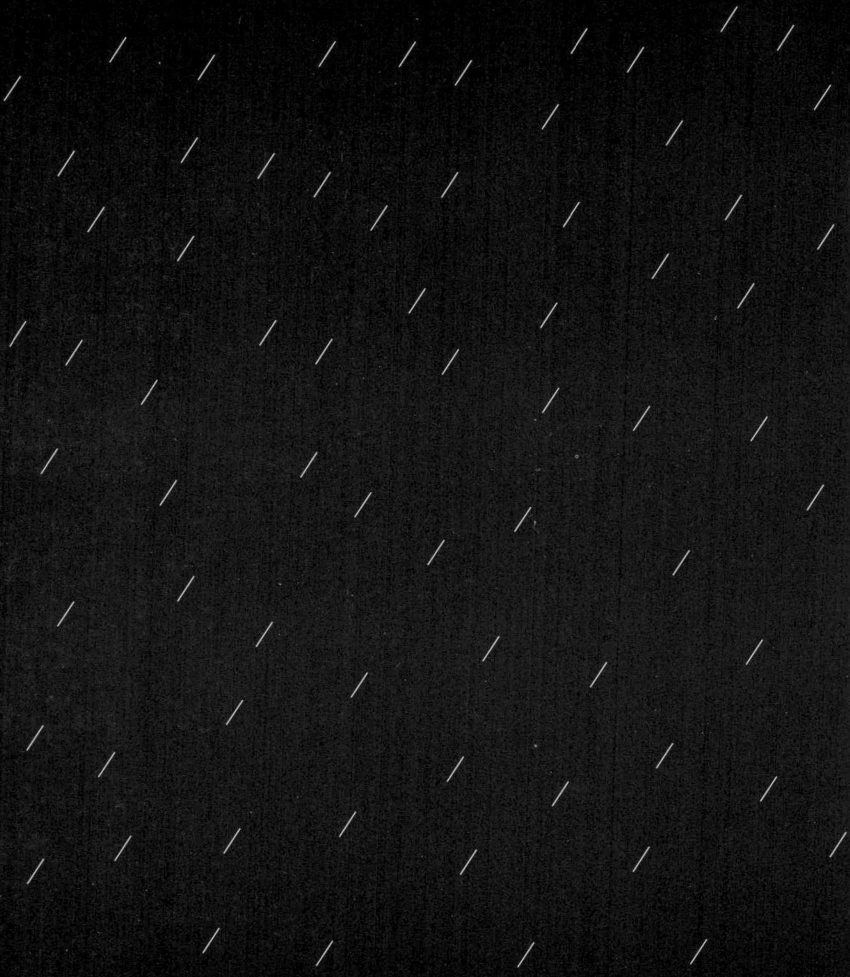

I watched the rain from the window. 'No stepping out,' Grandma said. But it was getting dark and there was so much to explore. I snuck out. It was quiet outside. The earth smelt good and the rain didn't hurt my head. I was muddy and wet when I got back. I had seen a weird little green snake and followed it into a bush; I had nearly caught a red-yellow dragonfly, and in my pocket was my big win — a bird-pecked guava that had swum to me through a puddle.

Grandma didn't like it. 'Dirty, dirty,' she muttered. She put a bucket of hot water in the bathroom and pointed to a clean towel. I took off my clothes and sat on a plastic bench beside the tap. I mixed hot water with cold till I got the right temperature. I got lost in the swirl of tap water falling into the bucket.

I felt a question rise up in me...

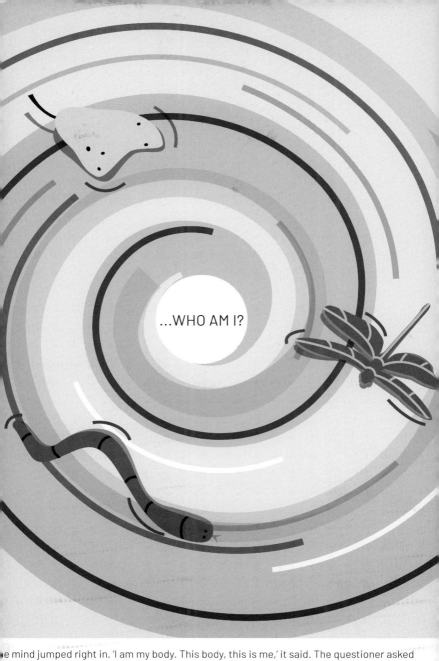

...WHO AM I?

The mind jumped right in. 'I am my body. This body, this is me,' it said. The questioner asked again, 'Who am I?' My gaze fell on my arms and legs. Goosebumps. My hands went up and scratched my head. The mind's answer hadn't hit the spot.

8.

UNDERSTANDING CONSCIOUSNESS: THE TRUE I

The electrical energy running through the toaster...

is the same as the one that's running through the steam iron...

the electric kettle...

the vacuum cleaner...

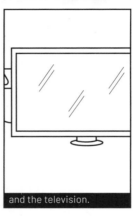

and the television.

But their circuitry and components are different.

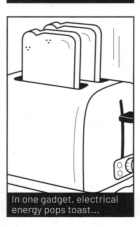

In one gadget, electrical energy pops toast...

in the other, it helps iron clothes...

and in another it produces moving images and sound.

Let's extend this to the human race.

Every human being is a uniquely designed instrument,
through which the same Primal Energy (or Source, or Consciousness
or God) functions.

This energy brings about whatever is supposed to happen
through each separate human instrument, every moment, according
to a cosmic law.

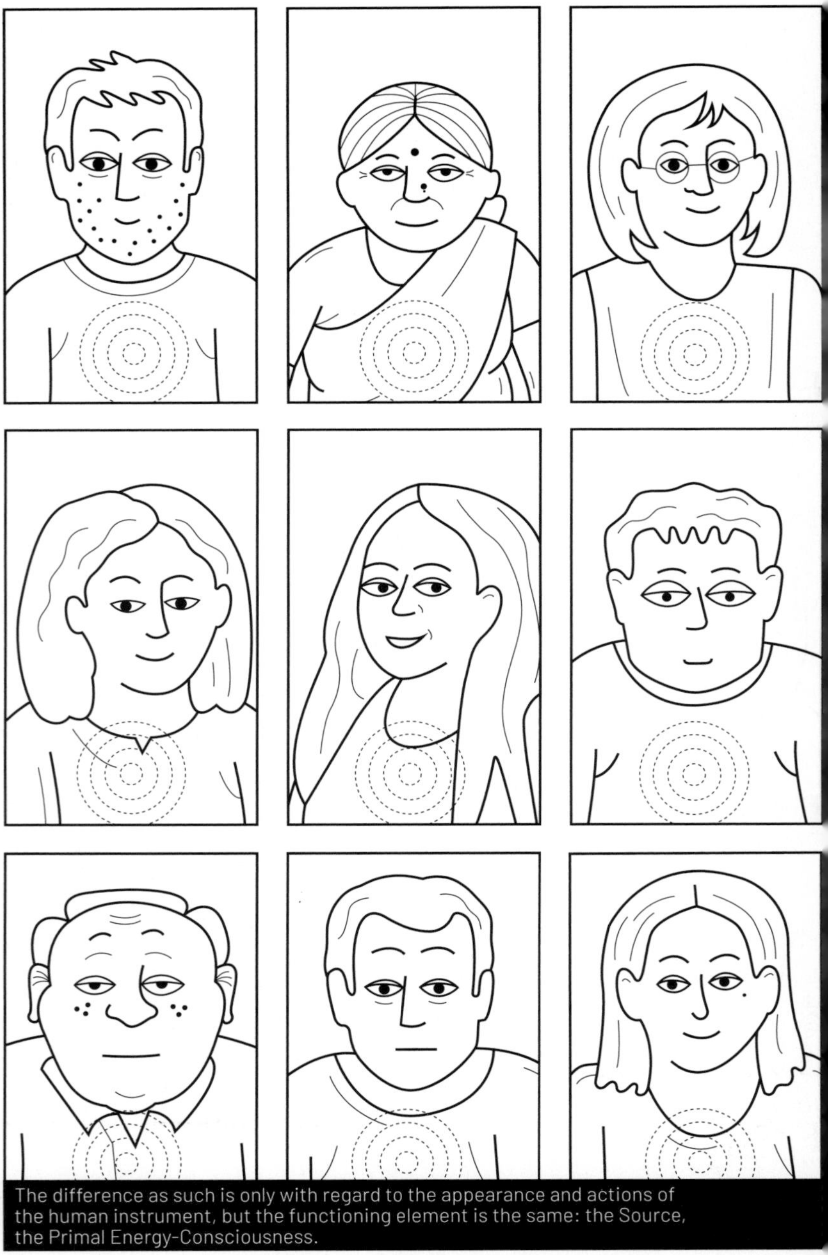

The difference as such is only with regard to the appearance and actions of the human instrument, but the functioning element is the same: the Source, the Primal Energy-Consciousness.

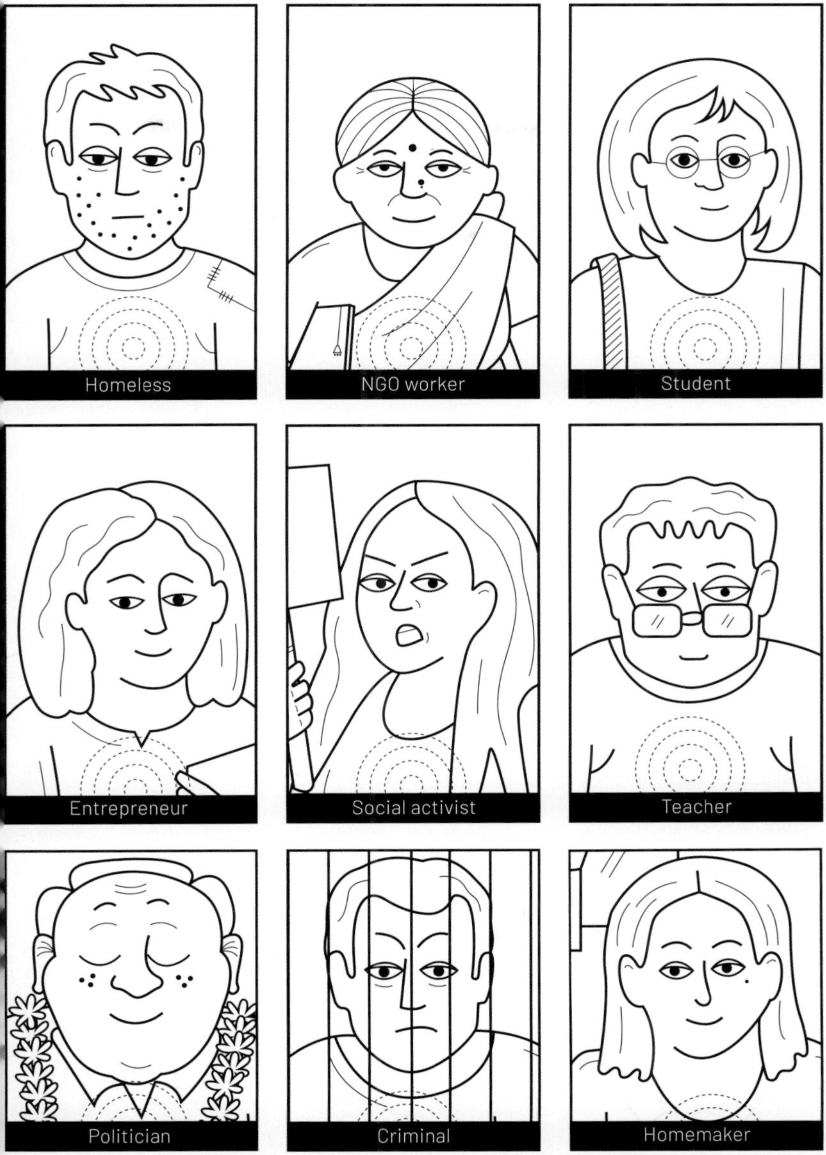
Homeless
NGO worker
Student
Entrepreneur
Social activist
Teacher
Politician
Criminal
Homemaker

This Primal Energy functions through each uniquely programmed human gadget precisely as electricity, an aspect of the same energy, functions through each electrical gadget, producing precisely what each electrical gadget is designed to produce.

So what is this Primal Energy, this Consciousness?

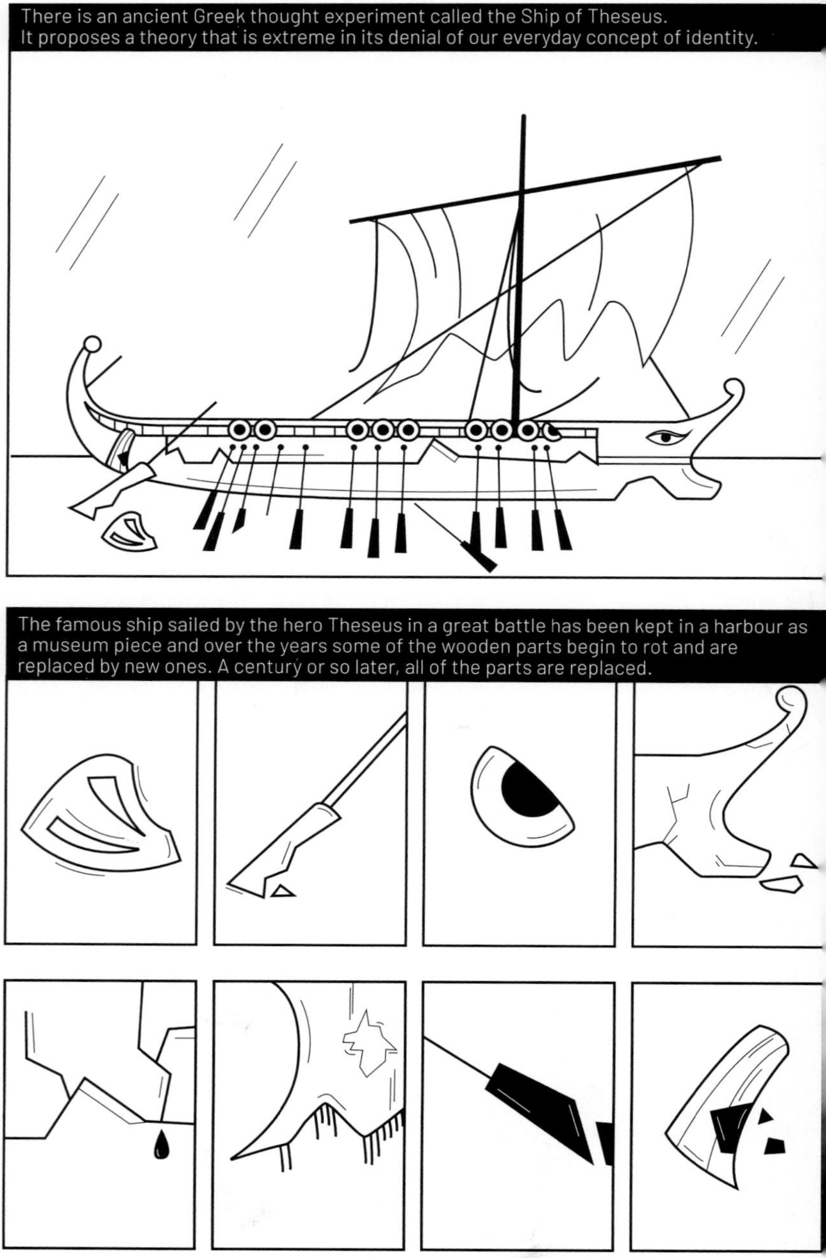
There is an ancient Greek thought experiment called the Ship of Theseus.
It proposes a theory that is extreme in its denial of our everyday concept of identity.
The famous ship sailed by the hero Theseus in a great battle has been kept in a harbour as a museum piece and over the years some of the wooden parts begin to rot and are replaced by new ones. A century or so later, all of the parts are replaced.

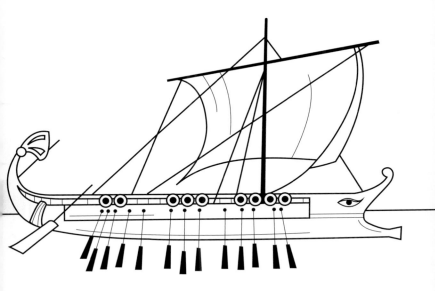

The question then is if the 'restored' ship is still the same object as the original.

According to the theory two ships, while identical in all the other ways, are not identical if they exist at two different times. Each ship-at-time is a unique 'event'.

So even without replacement of parts, the ships are different.

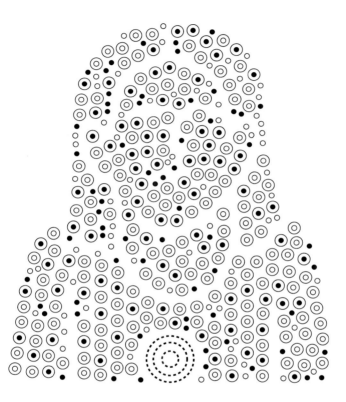

Let's take the individual, that is, the body-mind organism.

Every cell of this individual is changing every instant, it's ageing, decaying, growing, dying, new cells forming. So is the mind-body that was there a second ago the same as the one now, in this instant when every cell in it has undergone a change?

We consider ourselves and this world to be real but what's truly real? If we define reality as an absolute truth — as something that is, was, and will always be unchanged, unaffected — then is there something that's absolutely real?

Everything is like the Ship of Theseus, always changing, mutating, decaying, taking birth, and dying — always in a flux. Like a large rock that eventually turns into dirt and rubble over hundreds of years.

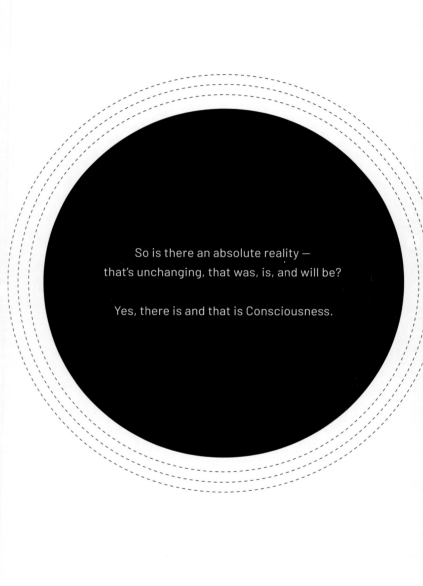

So is there an absolute reality —
that's unchanging, that was, is, and will be?

Yes, there is and that is Consciousness.

So can we perceive this Consciousness? Of course, it's always with us.

Right now, as you read this, the only truth that you can be absolutely certain of is that you exist.

Who is reading? Someone's reading and that someone is you.

But then Advaita says the 'I' or the 'you' doesn't exist. If 'I' doesn't exist then who is reading this page? Who is aware of the surroundings? Who is that which sees? Who is the witness?

Who is this 'I' and where does it come from?

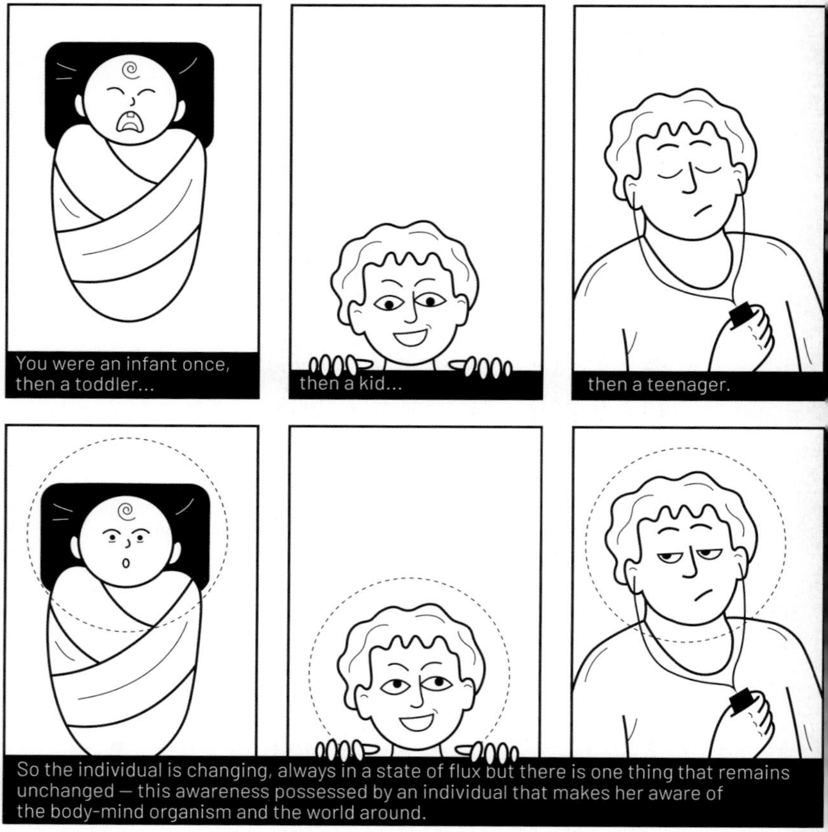
You were an infant once, then a toddler...
then a kid...
then a teenager.
So the individual is changing, always in a state of flux but there is one thing that remains unchanged — this awareness possessed by an individual that makes her aware of the body-mind organism and the world around.

This awareness is mistaken as 'I'.

The illusory 'I' has seen different things, felt different things, thought different things but the seer/the awareness/the Consciousness is constant. It's always there.

Now, this Consciousness can't be the 'I' defined by the mind. The mind keeps changing and evolving and decaying. It's not constant.

So the Consciousness we are looking for — the one that's constant and unchanging — is beyond the mind. It can be intuitively perceived if we withdrew our senses and stilled our thoughts.

Let's try this experiment when you have fifteen minutes of uninterrupted time to spare.

Sit in a room with minimal distractions.

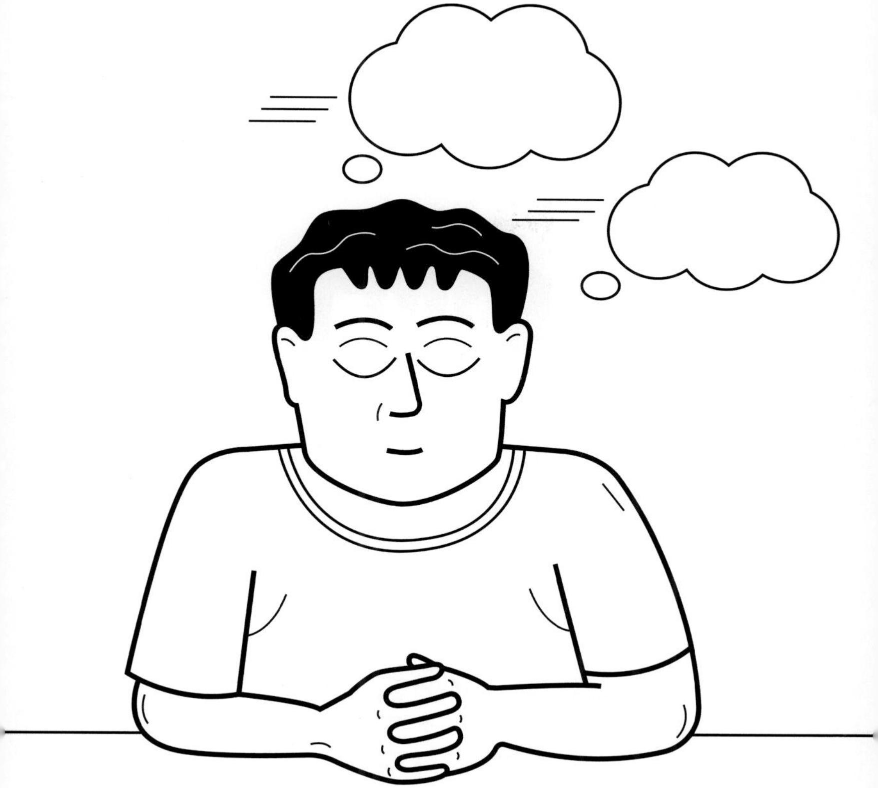

WITHDRAW FROM THE SENSE OF SIGHT

Adjust your eyes to the light in the room and then close your eyes.

If thoughts arise, observe them but don't flow (identify) with them. It's easier said than done but if you observe them without forming any opinion (just pure witnessing), then the thoughts will go away.

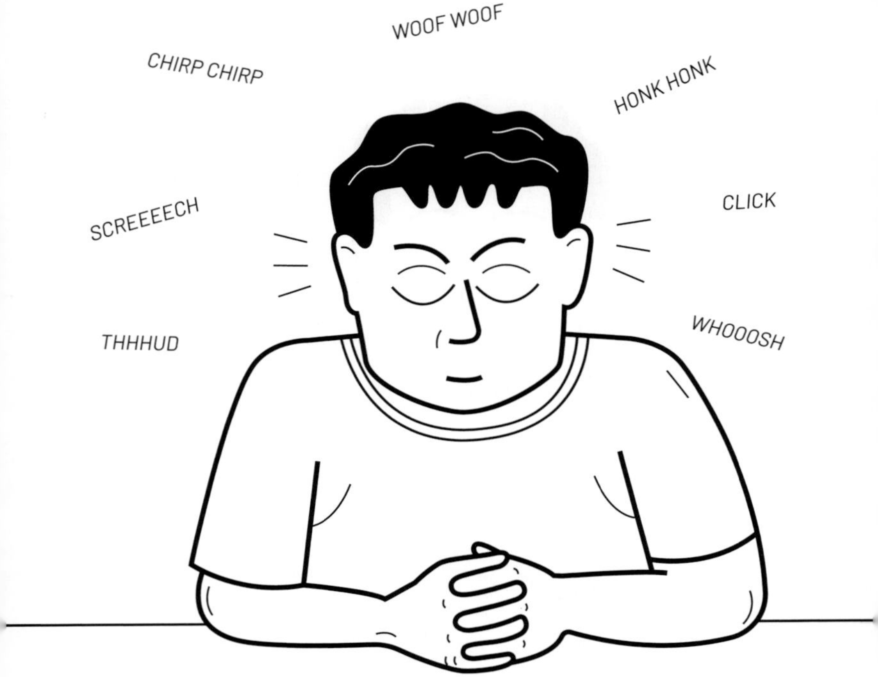
WOOF WOOF
CHIRP CHIRP
HONK HONK
SCREEEEECH
CLICK
THHHUD
WHOOOSH

WITHDRAW FROM THE SENSE OF HEARING

Hear all the sounds in the room and get accustomed to them. Don't interpret, don't label what you hear. If thoughts do arise, observe them but don't judge or flow (identify) with them. They will go away.

WITHDRAW FROM THE SENSE OF SMELL

Become comfortable with the smell in the room.
Don't interpret, don't label what you smell. If thoughts
do arise, observe them but don't judge or flow with them.
They will go away.

WITHDRAW FROM THE SENSE OF TOUCH

Feel your body on the couch or chair. Become comfortable
with all the things touching your body. Don't interpret, don't label
what you feel at the touch. If thoughts do arise, observe them
but don't judge or flow with them. They will go away.

WITHDRAW FROM THE SENSE OF TASTE

Familiarize yourself with the taste in your mouth.
Don't interpret, don't label what you taste.
If thoughts arise, observe them but don't judge
or flow with them. They will go away.

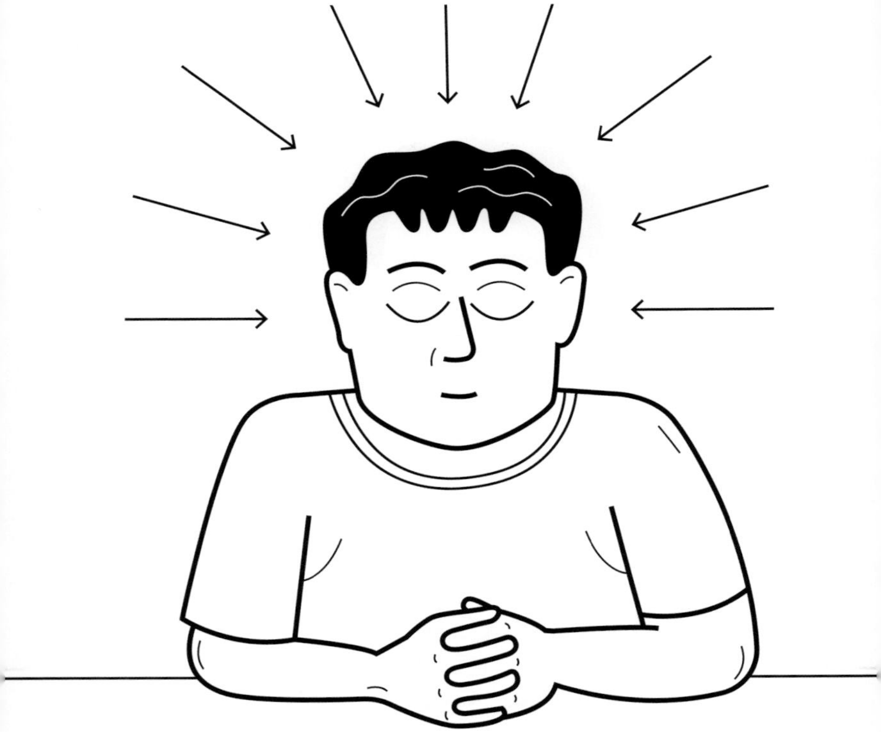

Withdraw your focus from the surroundings (senses) to the one who is aware of the surroundings.

Don't read further. Try it.

When you have withdrawn your focus from all externalizations
of the mind, then you will find emptiness.
No thought, no sense perceptions, just silence. Be here now.

This is a taste of pure consciousness. This is where we truly belong.

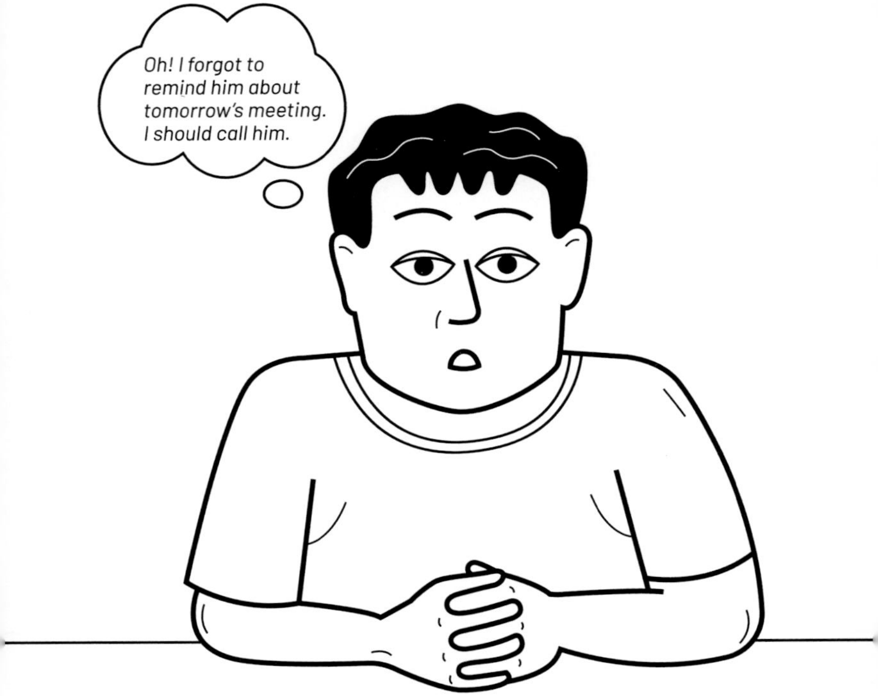
Oh! I forgot to remind him about tomorrow's meeting. I should call him.

Our conditioning makes it difficult for us to stay here for long but the few seconds of silence and quiet that you felt is probably your first formal introduction to pure awareness (or Consciousness).

This is the witness, the seer, the empty canvas on which your mind paints the pictures it does – past, future, worries, anxieties, the feeling of incompleteness, of joy and happiness – everything fleeting. The screen remains unchanged, unaffected but the scenes change and keep changing. Without the screen there are no images, there is no movie. But the screen is ever present, with or without the movie.

This is what all great teachers mean when they say we are all ONE, we are all equal. This is the answer to the question: Who am I?

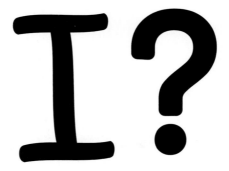

The purpose of all Advaita teaching is to get you in touch with this pure reality and guide you to stay absorbed in it instead of flowing with the ego-sense or 'I'.

Pure Consciousness is where the mind finds lasting peace. The mind's true abode is where it came from.

Consciousness is the only reality. Consciousness plus waking, we call waking. Consciousness plus sleep, we call sleep. Consciousness plus dream, we call dream. Consciousness is the screen on which all the pictures come and go. The screen is real, the pictures are mere shadows on it.

~ Ramana Maharshi

∞

The whole universe is a movement into consciousness.

~ Eckhart Tolle

PART 3

A NEW LIGHT

9.

HUMILITY & COMPASSION

The only true meaning of love is to know the 'other' as yourself.

~ Eckhart Tolle

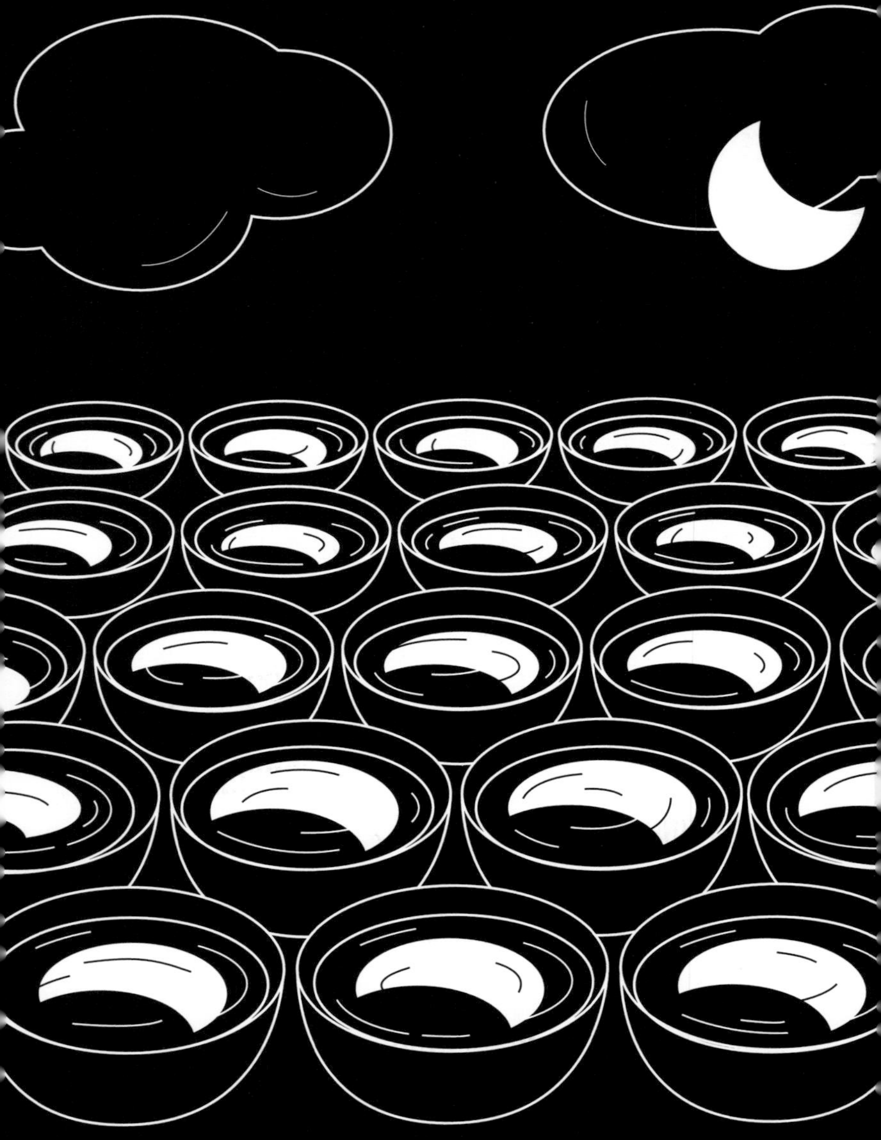

We are like vessels of water reflecting the same moon...the images are all different from each other but the moon remains unchanged. This unifying, universal Consciousness makes us all ONE (and even if we appear to be separated by our ego-sense, we are all equal).

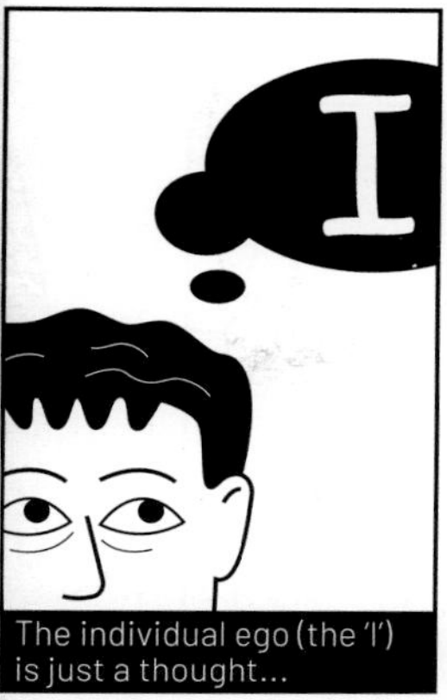
I
The individual ego (the 'I')
is just a thought...

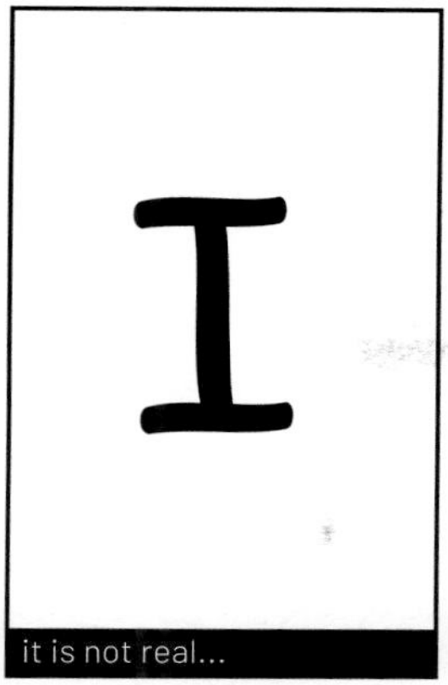
I
it is not real...

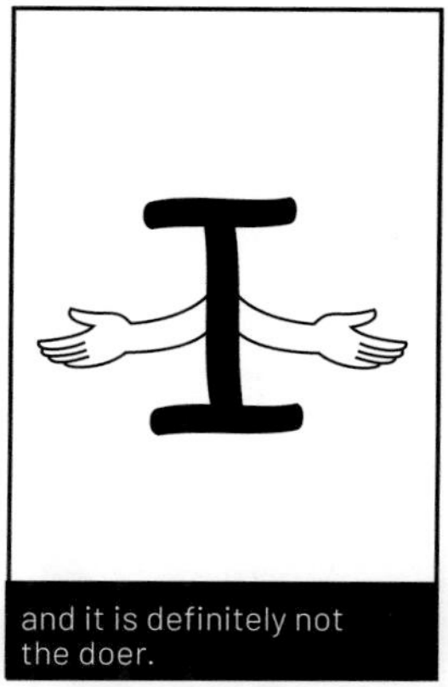
I
and it is definitely not
the doer.

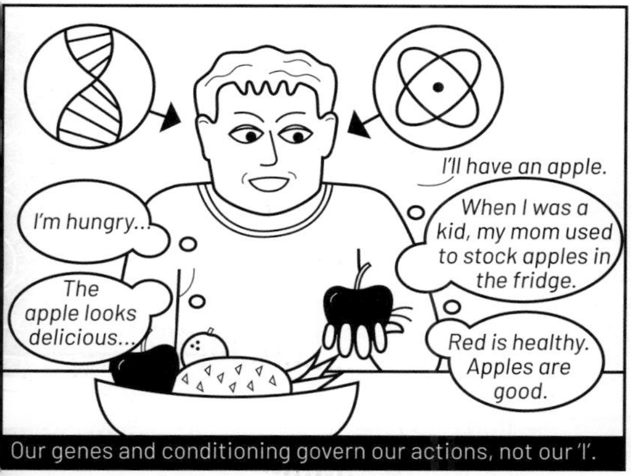
I'm hungry...
The apple looks delicious...
I'll have an apple.
When I was a kid, my mom used to stock apples in the fridge.
Red is healthy. Apples are good.
Our genes and conditioning govern our actions, not our 'I'.

This understanding can lead us to a few conclusions.

Floating in this discovery of being ONE with all, one can only become empathetic and compassionate (yes, that's conditioning that occurs post complete understanding). Hence, when we serve others, we are truly serving ourselves.

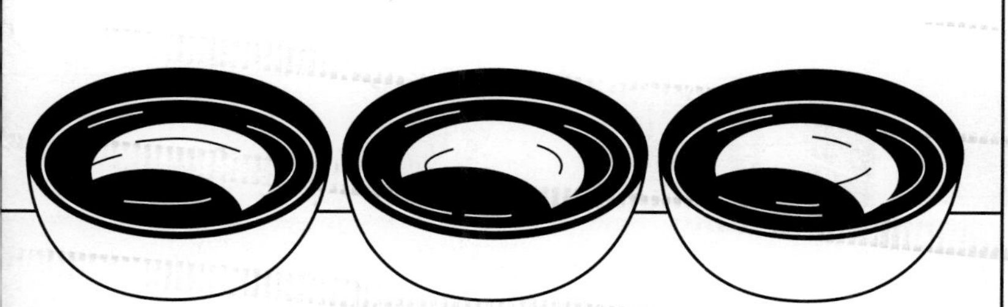

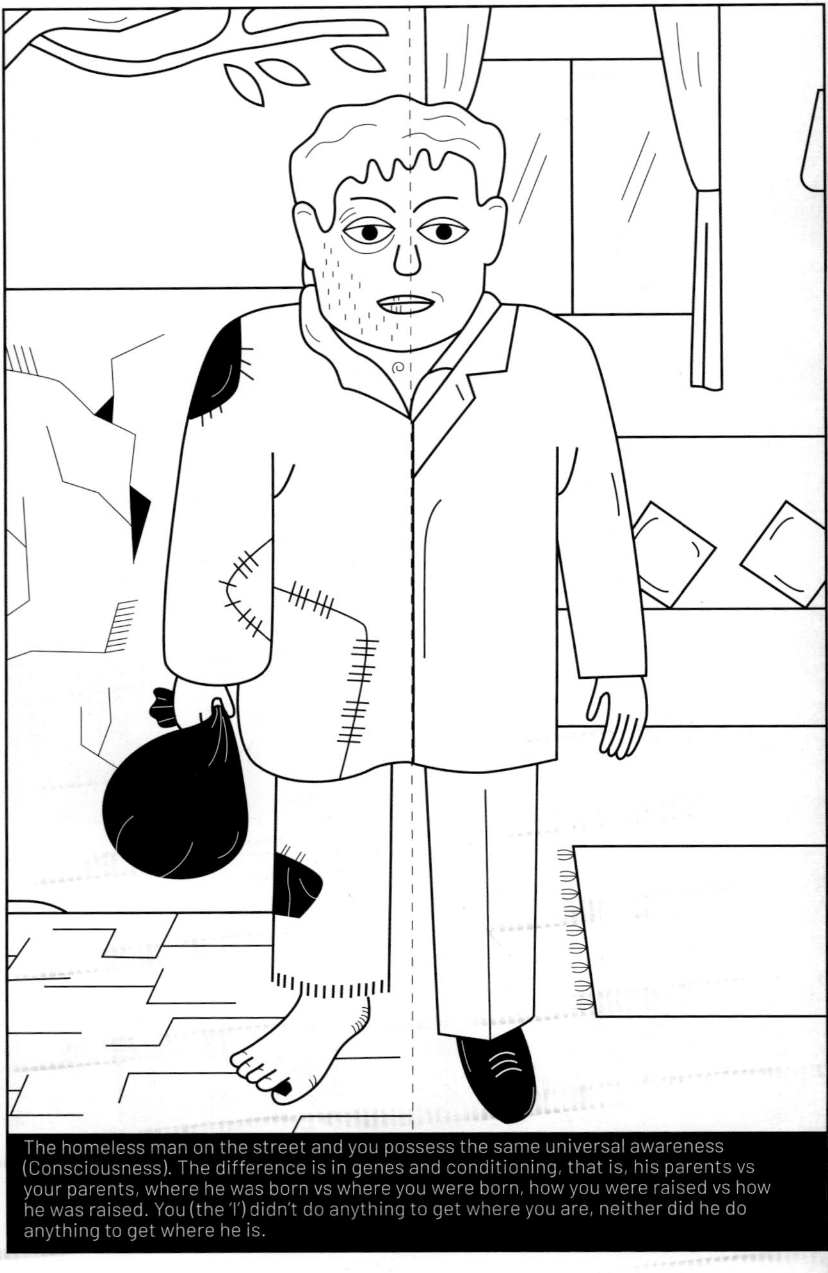

The homeless man on the street and you possess the same universal awareness (Consciousness). The difference is in genes and conditioning, that is, his parents vs your parents, where he was born vs where you were born, how you were raised vs how he was raised. You (the 'I') didn't do anything to get where you are, neither did he do anything to get where he is.

We are all one. This understanding should lead to total humility and compassion towards all living beings.

This humility and compassion is the genesis of all other great human qualities. If you ever want to know if someone is a sage, look for these traits.

10.

ACCEPTANCE

Without desire, resolve, or effort, the sun rises;
and, in its mere presence, the sunstone emits fire,
the lotus blooms, water evaporates,
people perform their various functions and then rest.

~ Ramana Maharshi

Life happens within you and without you, life happens as per God's will or a cosmic law. How and why things happen the way they do is beyond the human mind's comprehension. Acceptance is peace.

From: I did this. He did this. She will do that. I shouldn't have done that.
To: It is what it is. It's all happening as per God's will or cosmic law.

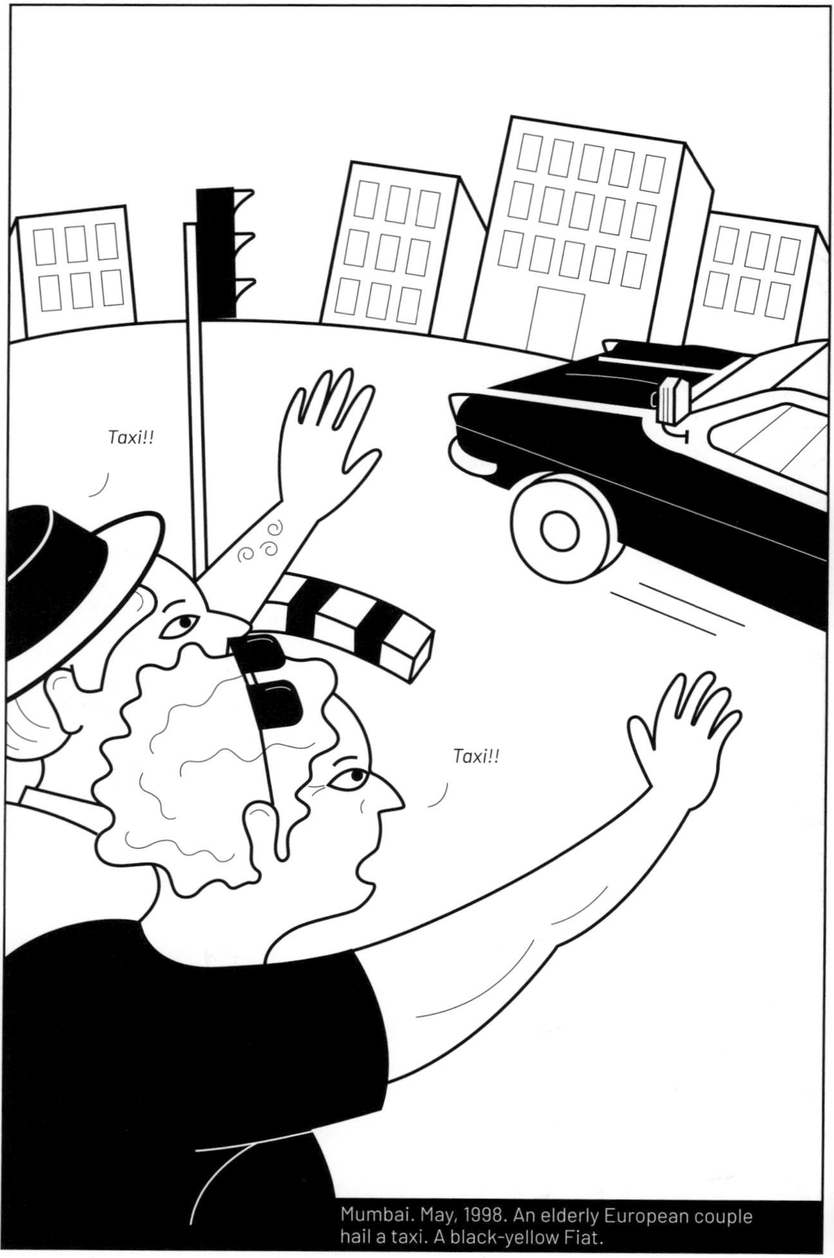
Taxi!!
Taxi!!
Mumbai. May, 1998. An elderly European couple hail a taxi. A black-yellow Fiat.

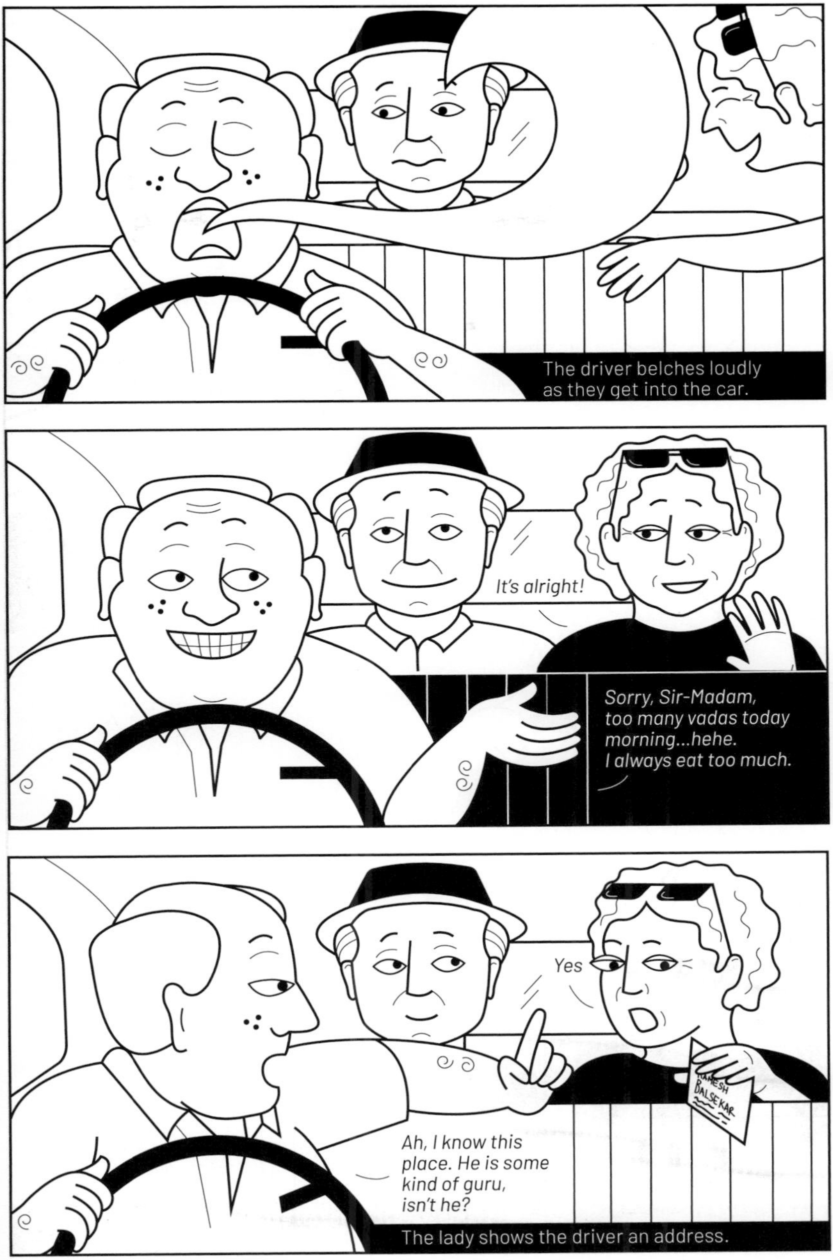

The driver belches loudly as they get into the car.
It's alright!
Sorry, Sir-Madam, too many vadas today morning...hehe. I always eat too much.
Yes
RAMESH BALSEKAR
Ah, I know this place. He is some kind of guru, isn't he?
The lady shows the driver an address.

Yes, okay but I don't know. These gurus and saints...

The driver lets out another one.

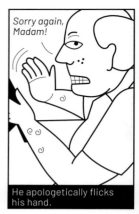

Sorry again, Madam!

He apologetically flicks his hand.

Sir-Madam, is it okay if I say something? I don't mean to offend you.

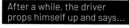

After a while, the driver props himself up and says...

Yes, yes. Say whatever you want to.

Can I come along? I mean, when you go to meet this guru, can I come too?

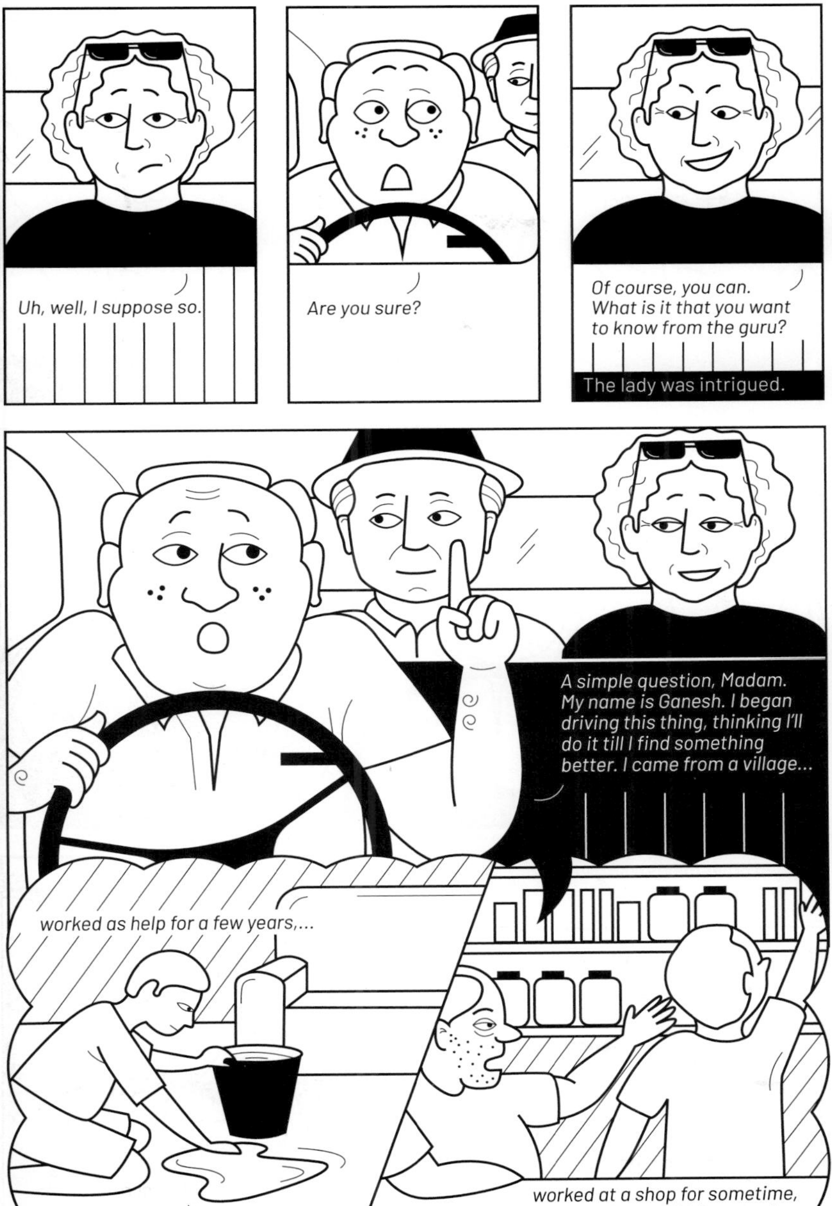

Uh, well, I suppose so.
Are you sure?
Of course, you can. What is it that you want to know from the guru?
The lady was intrigued.
A simple question, Madam. My name is Ganesh. I began driving this thing, thinking I'll do it till I find something better. I came from a village...
worked as help for a few years,...
worked at a shop for sometime, and then began driving a taxi.

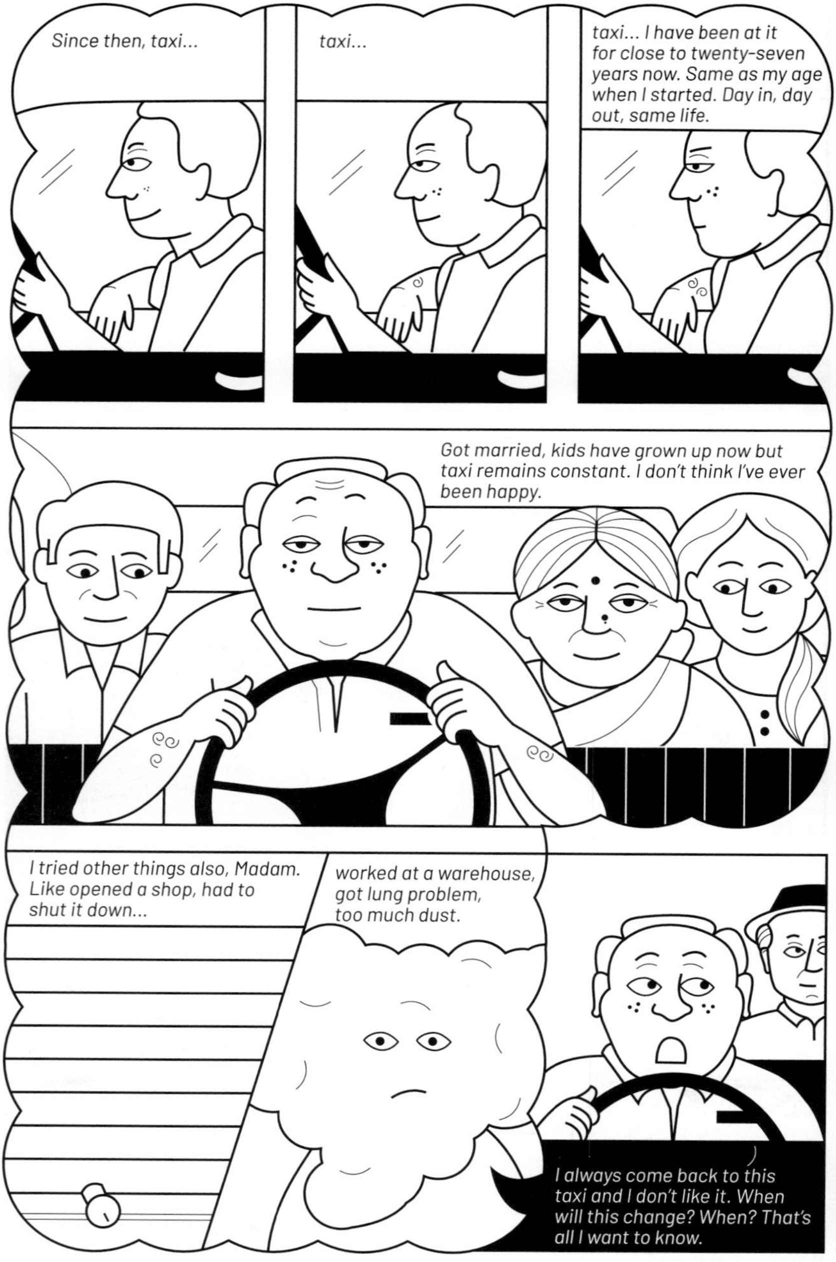
Since then, taxi...
taxi...
taxi... I have been at it for close to twenty-seven years now. Same as my age when I started. Day in, day out, same life.
Got married, kids have grown up now but taxi remains constant. I don't think I've ever been happy.
I tried other things also, Madam. Like opened a shop, had to shut it down...
worked at a warehouse, got lung problem, too much dust.
I always come back to this taxi and I don't like it. When will this change? When? That's all I want to know.

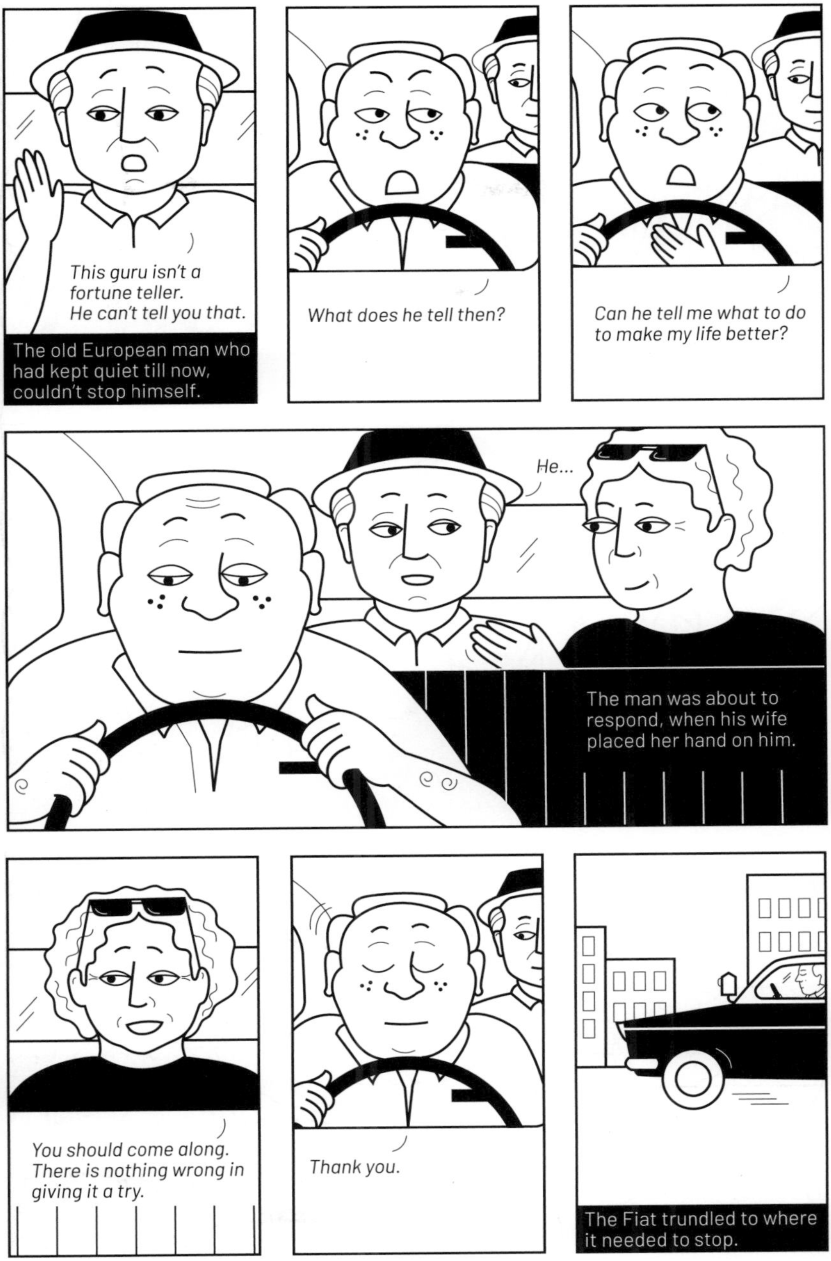
This guru isn't a fortune teller. He can't tell you that.
The old European man who had kept quiet till now, couldn't stop himself.
What does he tell then?
Can he tell me what to do to make my life better?
He...
The man was about to respond, when his wife placed her hand on him.
You should come along. There is nothing wrong in giving it a try.
Thank you.
The Fiat trundled to where it needed to stop.

They climbed up the stairs to a crowded loft. An old man was sitting on an arm chair. He was the centre of attention amongst a motley crowd of seekers.

The European couple and their driver greeted the old man...

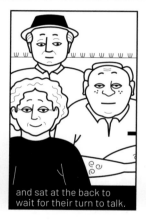

and sat at the back to wait for their turn to talk.

You ask your question. Don't be afraid, okay?

He nodded.

His turn came.

I began driving a taxi...

He repeated what he had told the couple earlier in the taxi.

Guru ji, I've been driving this taxi for twenty-seven years now. I have hated every minute of this life. What should I do? Can you give me something that can change things for me?

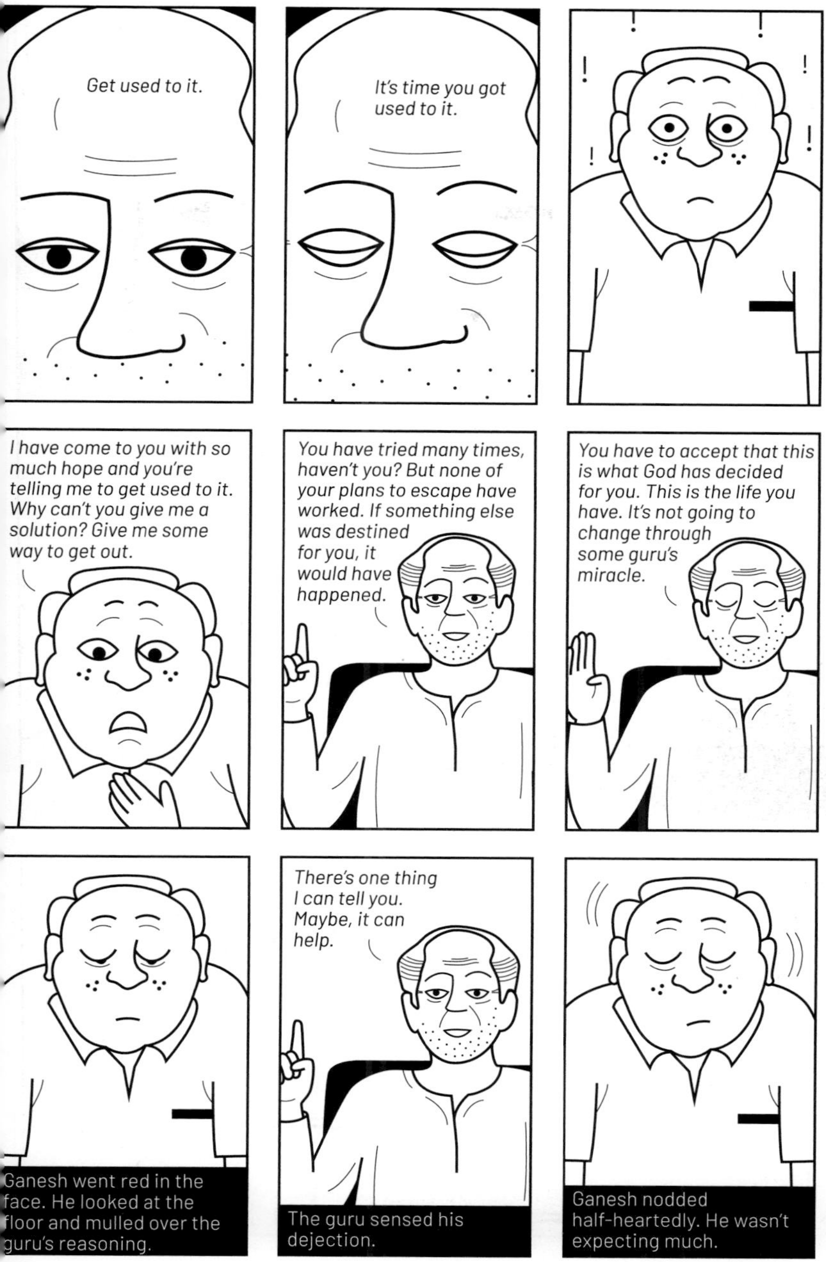
Get used to it.
It's time you got used to it.
I have come to you with so much hope and you're telling me to get used to it. Why can't you give me a solution? Give me some way to get out.
You have tried many times, haven't you? But none of your plans to escape have worked. If something else was destined for you, it would have happened.
You have to accept that this is what God has decided for you. This is the life you have. It's not going to change through some guru's miracle.
Ganesh went red in the face. He looked at the floor and mulled over the guru's reasoning.
There's one thing I can tell you. Maybe, it can help.
The guru sensed his dejection.
Ganesh nodded half-heartedly. He wasn't expecting much.

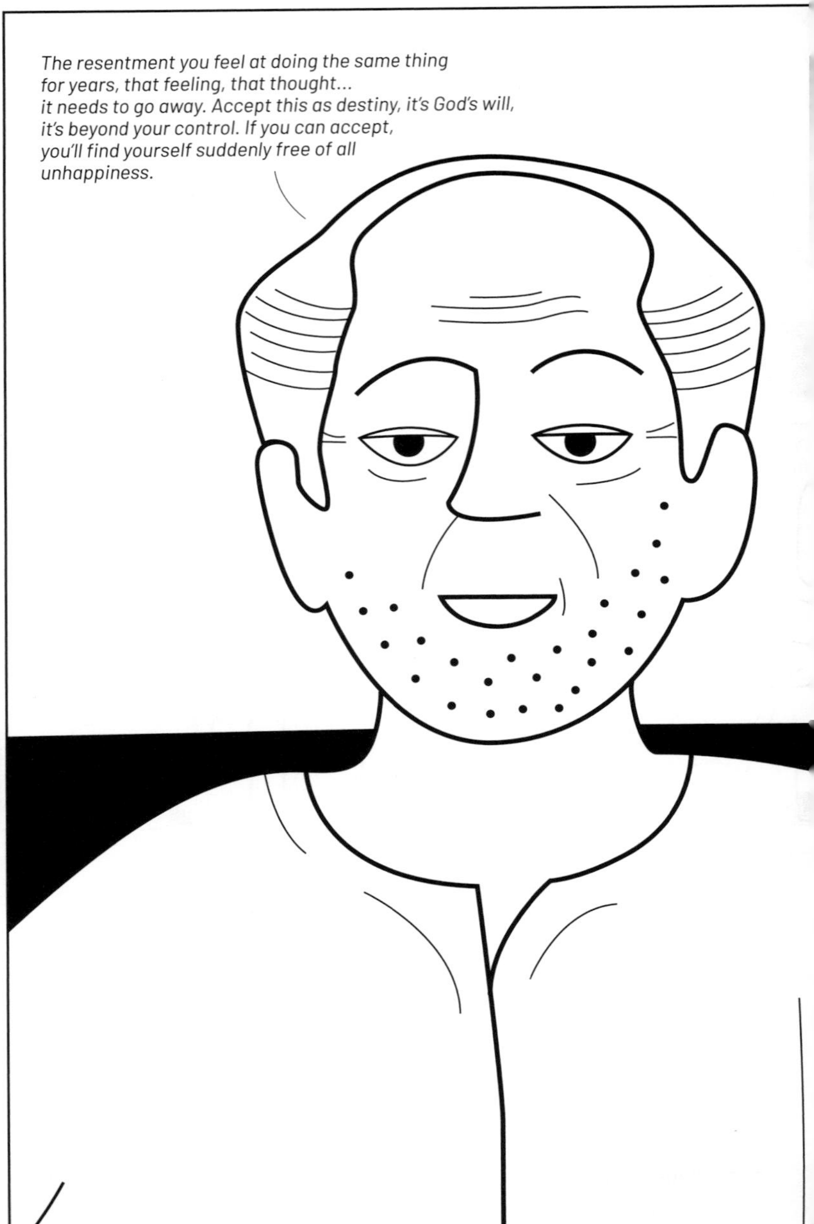
The resentment you feel at doing the same thing
for years, that feeling, that thought...
it needs to go away. Accept this as destiny, it's God's will,
it's beyond your control. If you can accept,
you'll find yourself suddenly free of all
unhappiness.

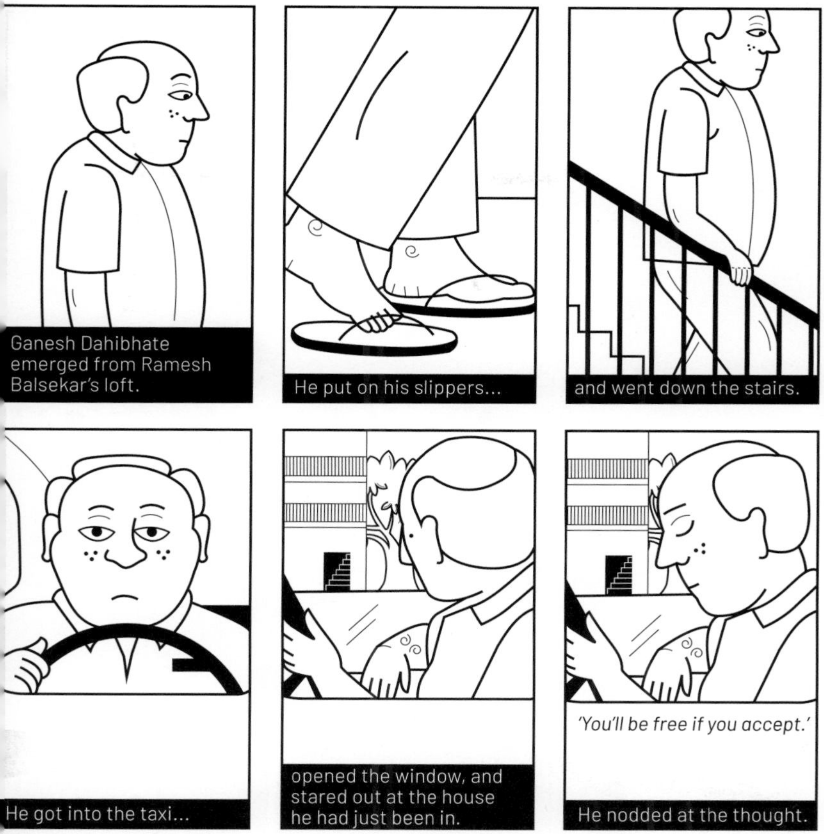
Ganesh Dahibhate emerged from Ramesh Balsekar's loft.
He put on his slippers...
and went down the stairs.
He got into the taxi...
opened the window, and stared out at the house he had just been in.
'You'll be free if you accept.'
He nodded at the thought.

Wouldn't we be at peace if we simply accepted the way things are instead of resisting or resenting it? But it's difficult because we believe things are the way they are because of what we did or what others have done and will do.

Getting rid of the false notion of doership opens the way to acceptance of what is. Acceptance of what is, is the way to liberation.

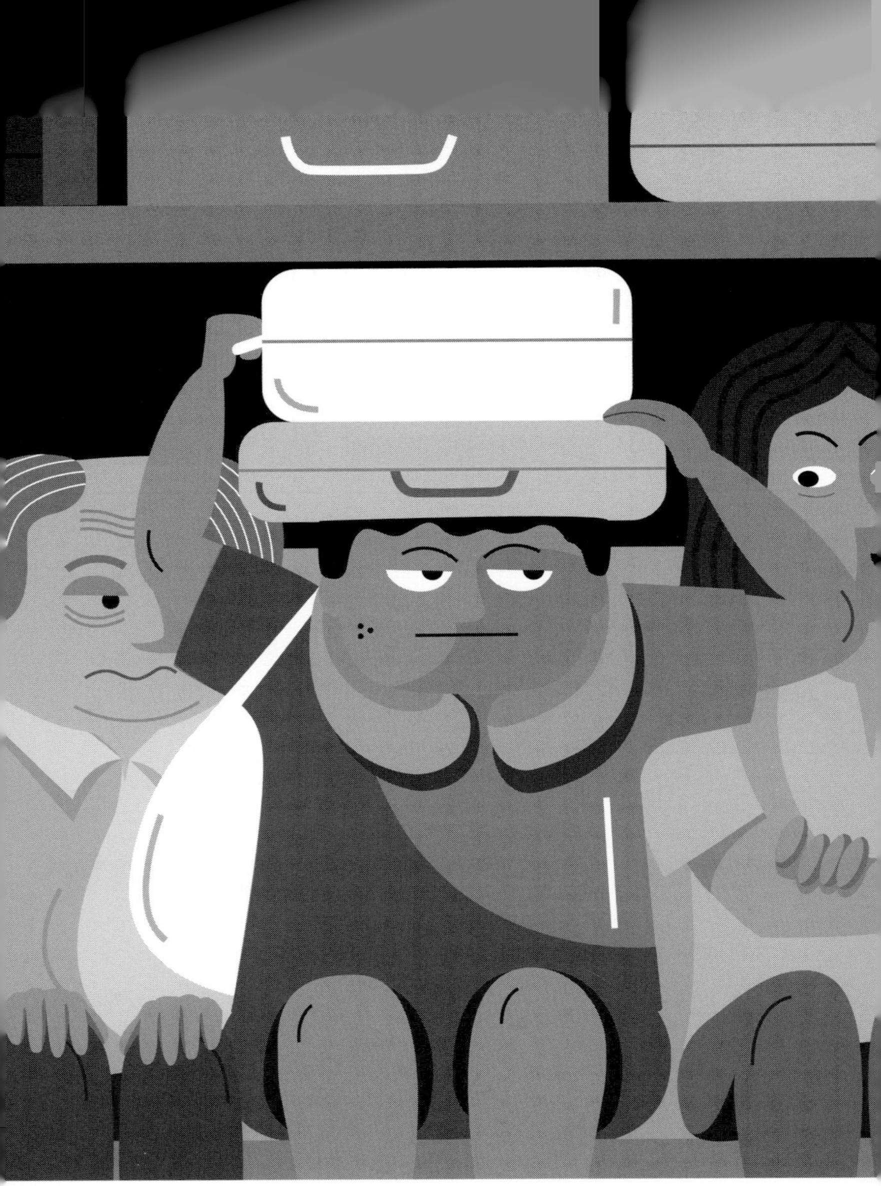

Whose fault is it if the traveller, instead of putting his luggage in the cart
which bears the load anyway, carries it on his head, to his own inconvenienc

~ Ramana Maharshi

PART 4

PRACTICES

A quick recap.

The 'I', or ego-sense, is the primary thought that identifies with the body-mind organism, that is, the 'I' creates the illusion that there is an individual that's 'other' than the rest of the world (separateness). This illusion leads to thoughts (because all thoughts are in relation to this individual). The 'I' also assumes false doership, that is, the delusion that this individual ('I') can make choices and do things.

We must realize that (a) the 'I' is not the doer (all actions and thoughts are outcomes of genes and conditioning); and (b) the 'I' doesn't exist. It is a faux layer that hides the truth or reality of consciousness/pure awareness/primal energy.

This pure awareness is our true nature. This is who we really are. The cashier at the supermarket, the stray dog, the pig in the sty, and the pebble in the garden, all are the same awareness: Consciousness.

However, people live under the tremendous weight of the false 'I' — a heaviness that stops us from attaining peace of mind. Hence, we must unravel the 'I' and go beyond it to pure awareness. This is where peace is, this is where we can find true freedom beyond anxieties, worries, and regrets.

People struggle with the acceptance that the 'I' isn't real. That's where most seekers hit a roadblock. In this part, we will talk about a few concepts and practices that can be applied to overcome this obstacle in order to attain a deeper experience of peace and happiness.

11.

RAMESH BALSEKAR'S ANALYSIS OF ACTIONS

Events happen, deeds are done but there is no individual doer.

~ Ramesh Balsekar

Non-doership, once understood and accepted, is an effective way to quieten the mind. If the ego-sense or 'I' is not the doer then thoughts are pointless and needn't be pursued. But completely dismissing individual doership is really difficult (since it's so deeply engrained in us due to lifelong conditioning).

Ramesh Balsekar recommended an analysis of one's actions as an effective way of realizing that the ego is not really in control. This interesting practice is initiated by the ego, and in the process the ego itself gets weakened.

Balsekar asked us to observe closely our day-to-day lives. Here's his example of a hungry man who needs to find some place to eat.

I'm hungry. I want to eat something.

I don't have much money so I want to find a clean restaurant where I will get reasonably good food at a reasonable price.

Is there a place?

Sure, just around the corner.

So he asks someone.

So what happened? There was a series of thoughts. The man's brain responded to those thoughts according to circumstances over which he had no control.

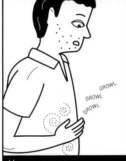

GROWL GROWL GROWL

Hunger arose...

he likes good and clean food, due to his conditioning...

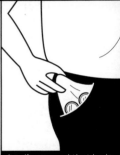

he discovered that he had very little money.

Is there a place where I can go?

Sure, just around the corner.

So the brain reacted to the existing situation and sought help from a stranger.

So how much was it 'his' action and how much was it a chain of circumstances and conditioning that led him to that restaurant?

When observed closely (and with practise), you come to the conclusion that it was not 'his' action.

'I' was suddenly hungry, and 'I' was led to a restaurant by a set of circumstances over which 'I' had no control.

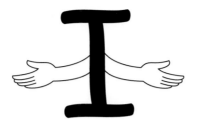

Ramesh is suggesting that we review events that occurred during the day and see our actions from the perspective of how much of it was in our control ('our' here implies the ego-sense or 'I').

While we are acting, we do feel we are in control. That's why he wants us to review our actions at the end of the day and not at the time when the action is taking place. There are two key things that need to be observed for this practice to be effective:

1. The focus is on analyzing actions and how they came about
   (do not delve too much on emotions and feelings)

2. The analysis has to be done at the end of the day
   (and not during the time when the actions occur)

This practice (or sadhana) is aimed at erasing our pre-programmed conditioning that takes 'I' as the doer.

Once I know I'm not the doer of actions being performed by my mind-body, I need to then ask a simple question: if I don't do anything, then who am I?

That's where Ramana Maharshi's Self-enquiry comes in.

12.

RAMANA MAHARSHI'S PRACTICE OF SELF-ENQUIRY

In order, therefore, to gain that happiness which is
one's (true) nature and which is experienced in the state of deep
sleep, where there is no mind, one should know oneself.

To achieve this, the Path of Knowledge,
the enquiry in the form of 'Who am I?', is the principal means.

~ *Who am I?* Ramana Maharshi

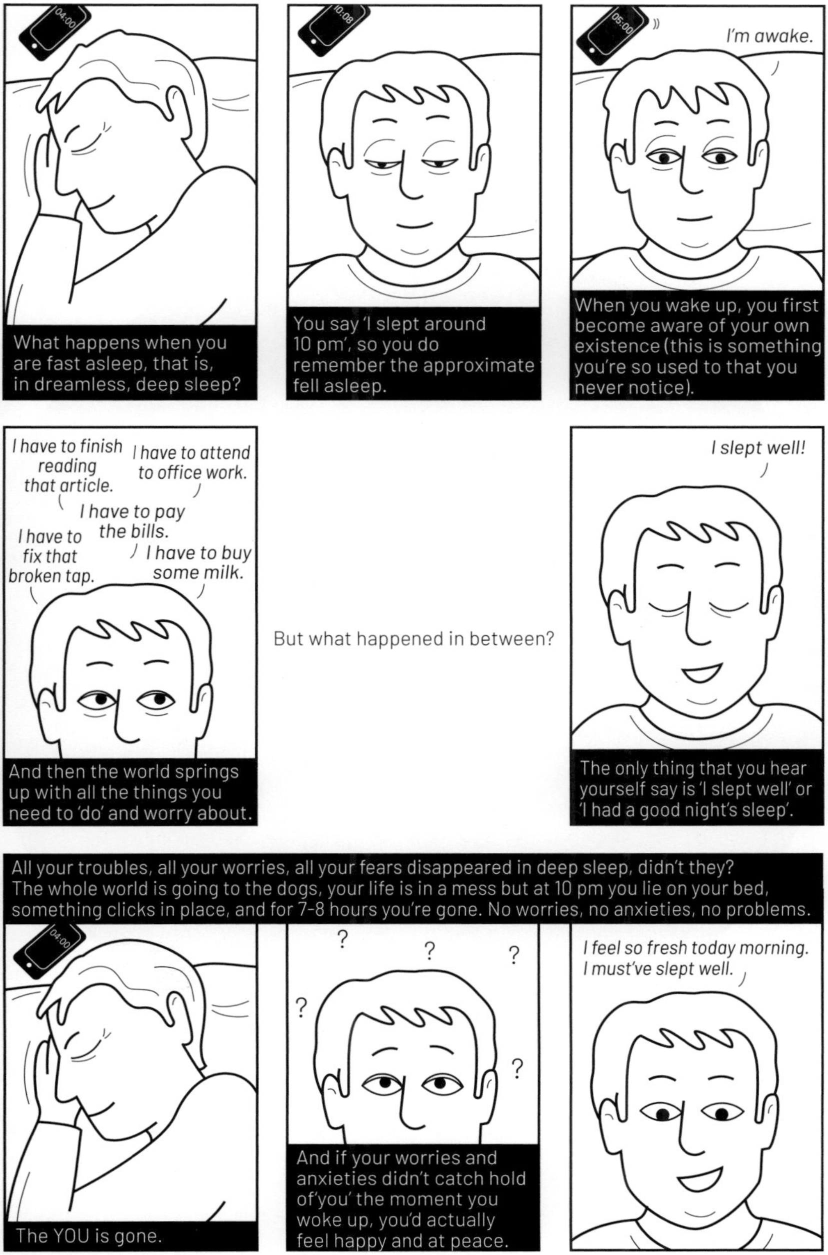

04:00
What happens when you are fast asleep, that is, in dreamless, deep sleep?
10:08
You say 'I slept around 10 pm', so you do remember the approximate
fell asleep.
05:00
I'm awake.
When you wake up, you first become aware of your own existence (this is something you're so used to that you never notice).
I have to finish reading that article.
I have to attend to office work.
I have to pay the bills.
I have to fix that broken tap.
I have to buy some milk.
And then the world springs up with all the things you need to 'do' and worry about.
But what happened in between?
I slept well!
The only thing that you hear yourself say is 'I slept well' or 'I had a good night's sleep'.
All your troubles, all your worries, all your fears disappeared in deep sleep, didn't they?
The whole world is going to the dogs, your life is in a mess but at 10 pm you lie on your bed, something clicks in place, and for 7-8 hours you're gone. No worries, no anxieties, no problems.
04:00
The YOU is gone.
? ? ? ? ?
And if your worries and anxieties didn't catch hold of'you' the moment you woke up, you'd actually feel happy and at peace.
I feel so fresh today morning. I must've slept well.

So, what happens in deep sleep?

In deep sleep, there is no mind (no 'I'). All worldly (external) layers are shed and our true Self (pure consciousness) shines forth. Ramana Maharshi would often give the example of deep sleep as to how happiness and peace are experienced every day by human beings.

But what about the waking state, that is,
the life that we have to live every day?

We know that past and future thoughts (thinking mind) are useless. These thoughts arise to a primary entity 'I' that doesn't exist; and these thoughts also assume doership of this non-existent 'I' (while in truth, there is no doer).

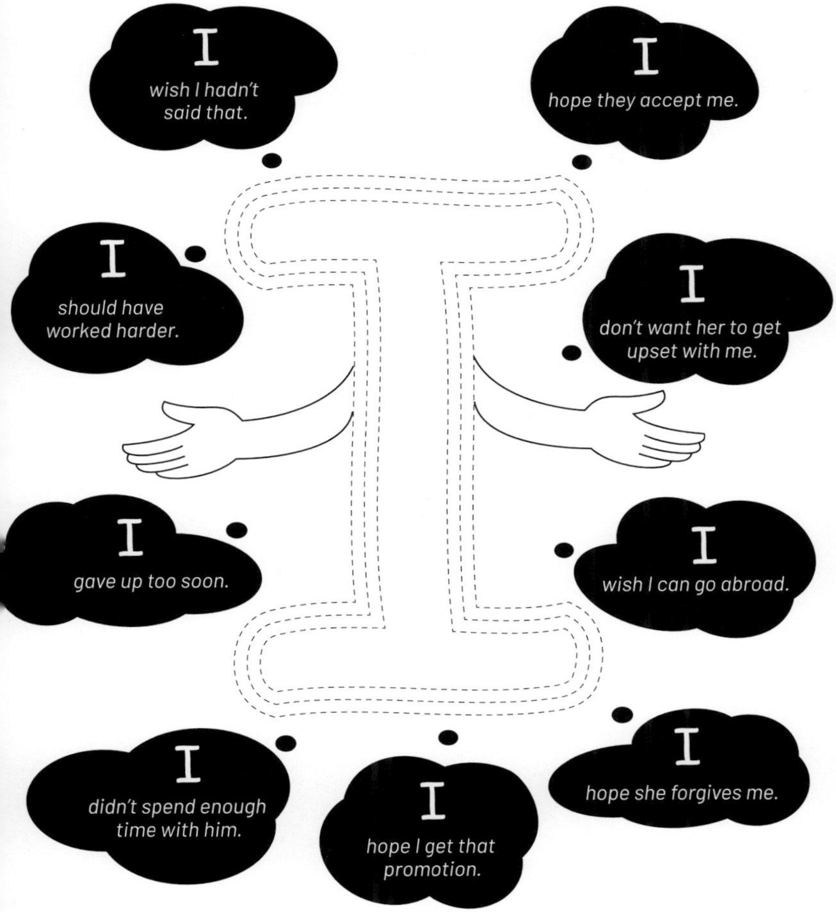
I
wish I hadn't said that.
I
hope they accept me.
I
should have worked harder.
I
don't want her to get upset with me.
I
gave up too soon.
I
wish I can go abroad.
I
didn't spend enough time with him.
I
hope I get that promotion.
I
hope she forgives me.

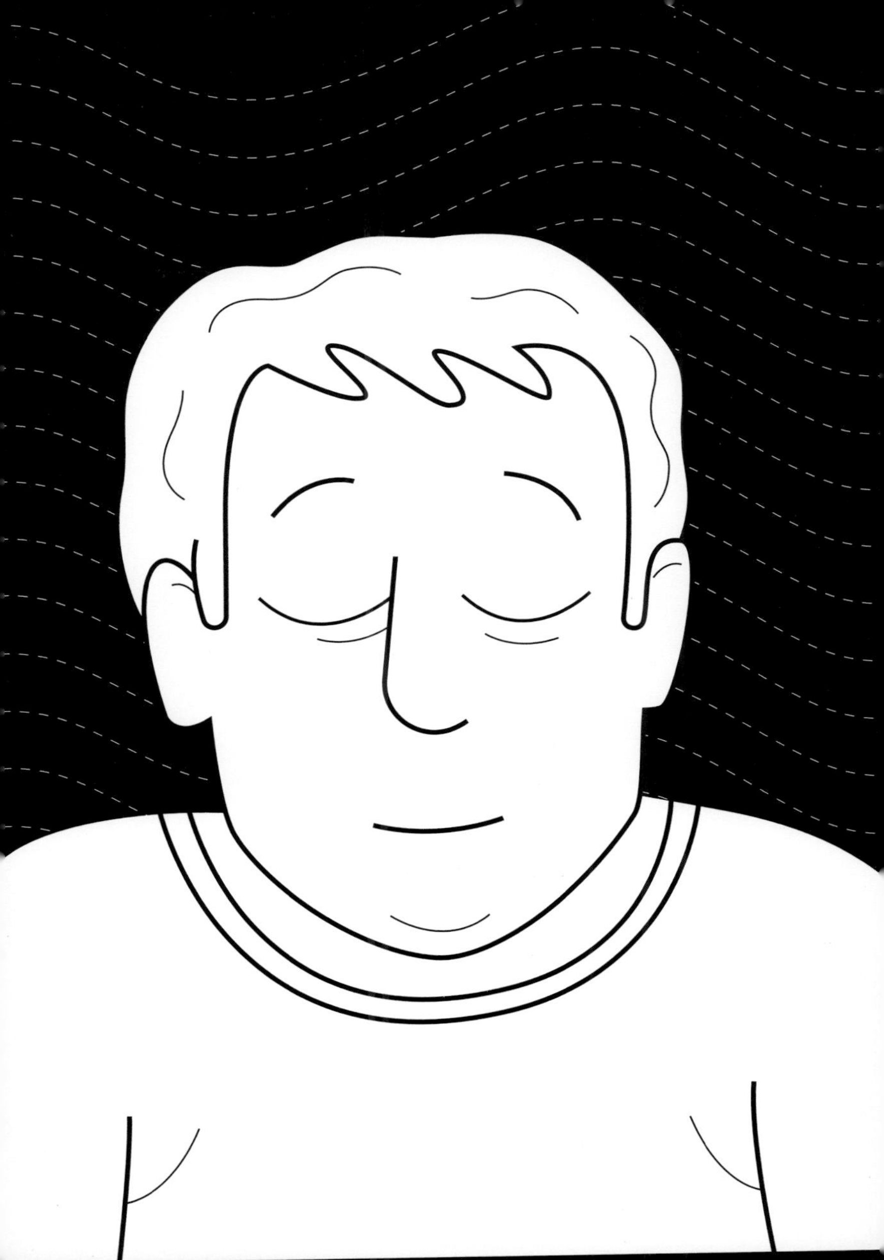

True happiness and peace are attained by residing in one's true nature. Having 'no mind' or no 'I'. We have to figure out a way to quieten the mind. That is why human beings invented meditation, breath control, and chanting — all tools to reduce thinking and quieten the mind.

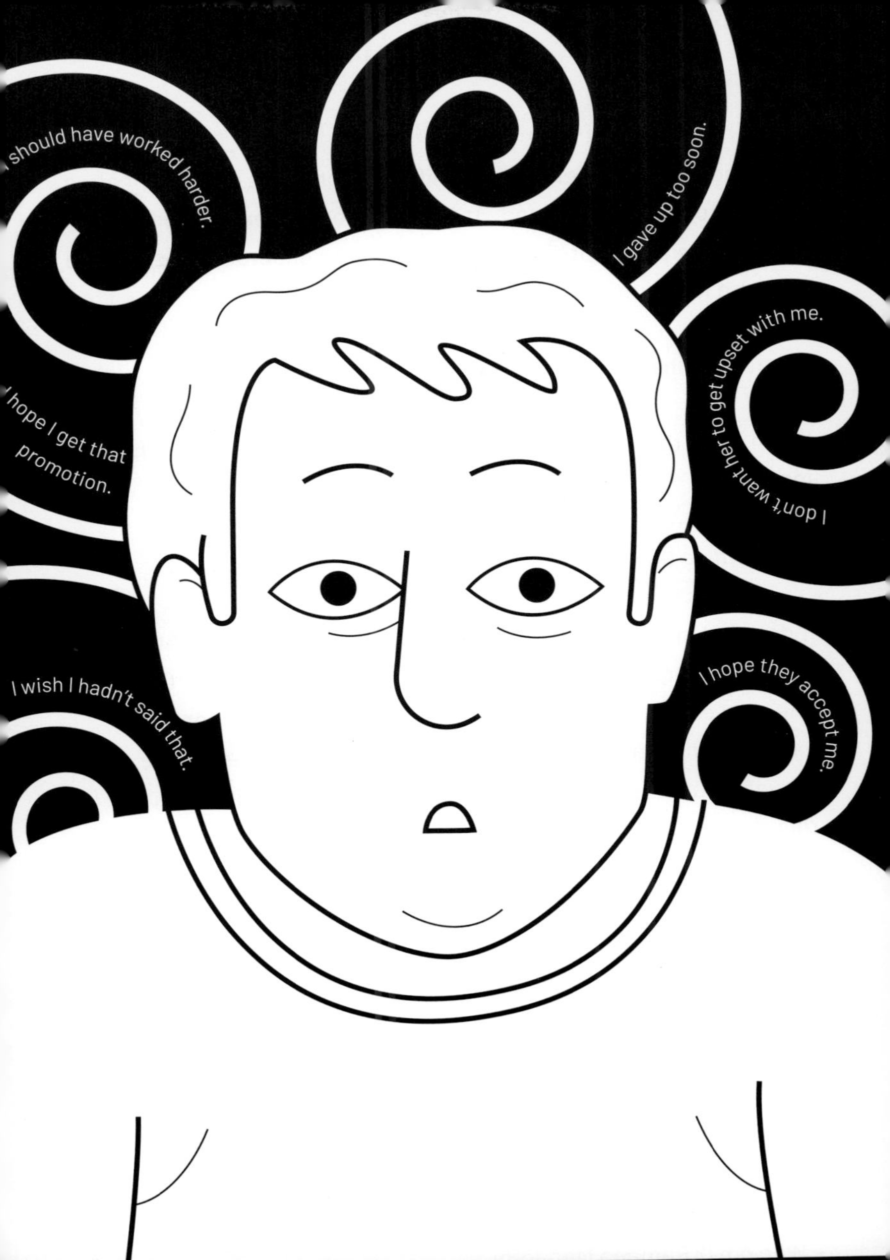
should have worked harder.
I gave up too soon.
I don't want her to get upset with me.
hope I get that promotion.
I wish I hadn't said that.
I hope they accept me.

The only challenge with all these practices is the mind that had quietened during practice goes about wreaking havoc as usual once the practice is over. If only we could stay in the thoughtless state all the time. That's where Ramana Maharshi's Self-enquiry can help.

The practice of 'Self-enquiry' is a life-long practice and an effective method to quieten the mind. At first glance, Self-enquiry appears straightforward but its subtleties need to be understood before the practice is begun.

Here's how the Maharshi describes Self-enquiry:

When other thoughts arise, one should not pursue them, but should inquire:

'To whom do they arise?'

It does not matter how many thoughts arise. As each thought arises, one should inquire with diligence, 'To whom has this thought arisen?' The answer that would emerge would be 'to me'. Thereupon if one inquires 'Who am I?', the mind will go back to its source and the thought that arose will become quiescent. With repeated practise in this manner, the mind will develop the skill to stay in its source.

When the mind that is subtle goes out through the brain and the sense-organs, the gross names and forms appear; when it stays in the heart, the names and forms disappear. Not letting the mind go out, but retaining it in the Heart is what is called 'inwardness' (antarmukha). Letting the mind go out of the Heart is known as 'externalization' (bahirmukha). Thus, when the mind stays in the Heart, the 'I' which is the source of all thoughts will go, and the Self which ever exists will shine.

~ *Who am I?* Ramana Maharshi

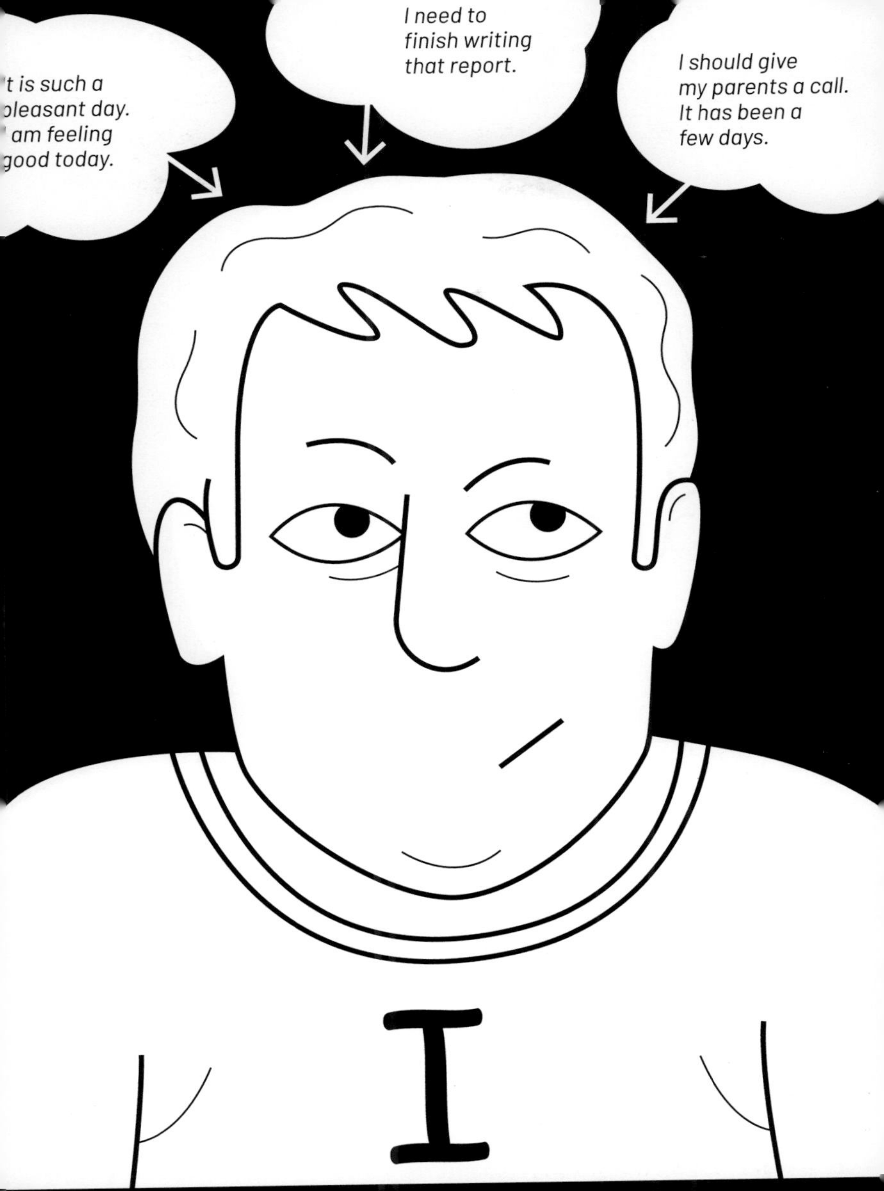
t is such a
leasant day.
am feeling
good today.
I need to finish writing that report.
I should give my parents a call. It has been a few days.
I

When we observe thoughts and ask, 'To whom do these thoughts occur?', the response is immediate: these thoughts occur to 'me'. In other words, who is thinking? Of course it's [redacted]

Who is this ‘me’?

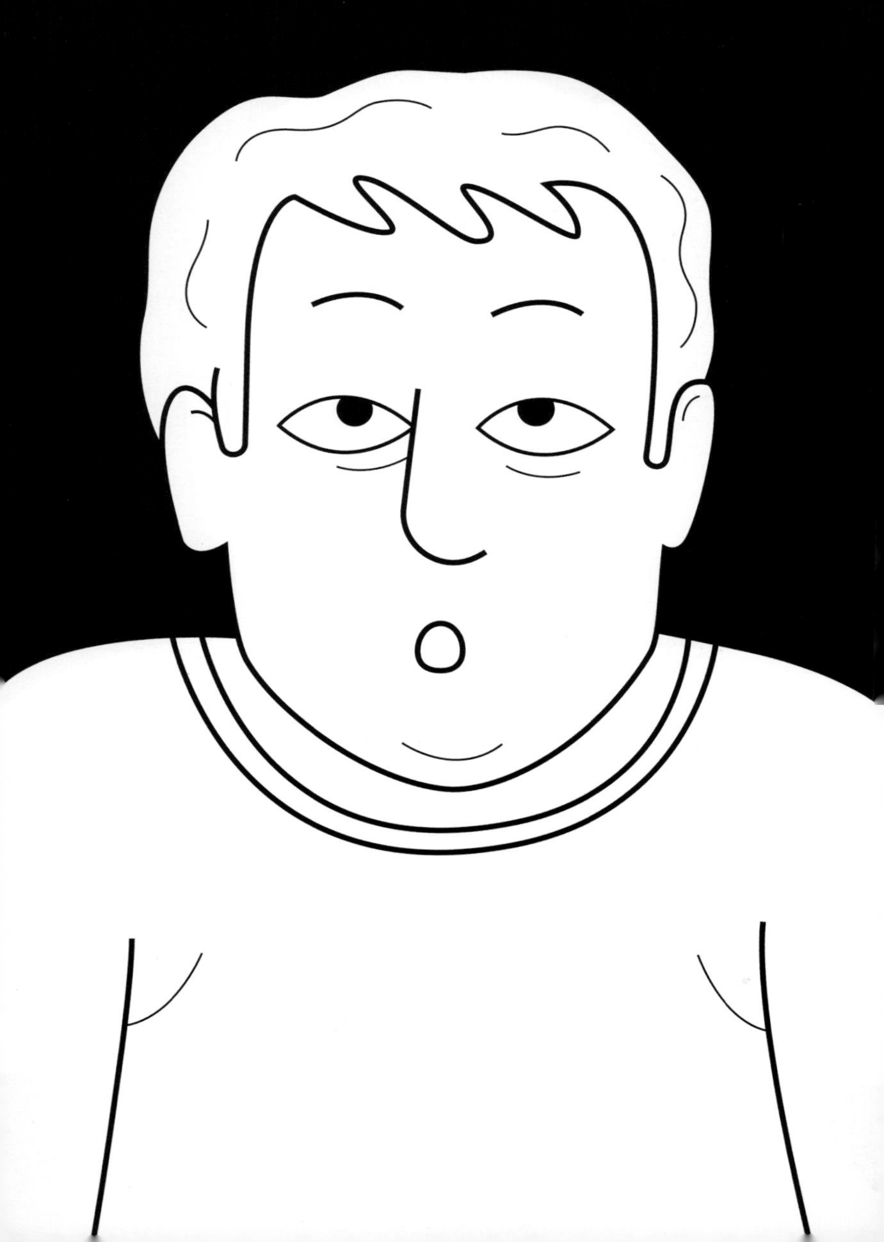

Asking this question can occur in two ways.

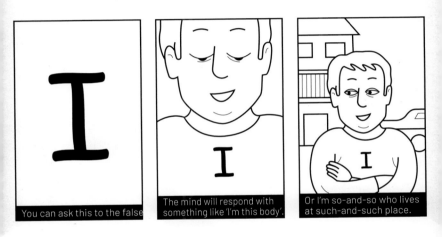

You can ask this to the false

The mind will respond with something like 'I'm this body'.

Or I'm so-and-so who lives at such-and-such place.

But that's not what Maharshi is asking us to do.

He is keen on taking us inward — there is no need for the mind to answer this question (which is tempting because it is conditioned to do so). This question needs to be asked to the source itself (to the Self or pure consciousness).

It is like peeling all the layers of the world

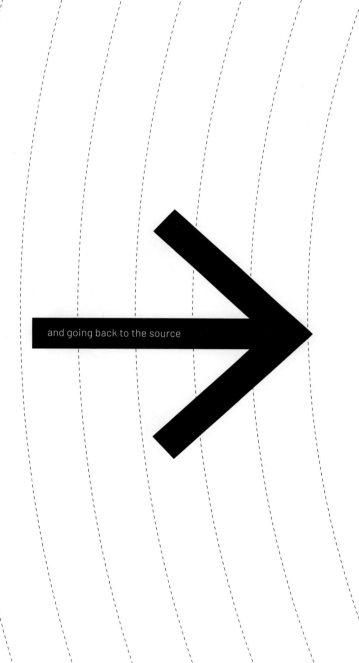
and going back to the source

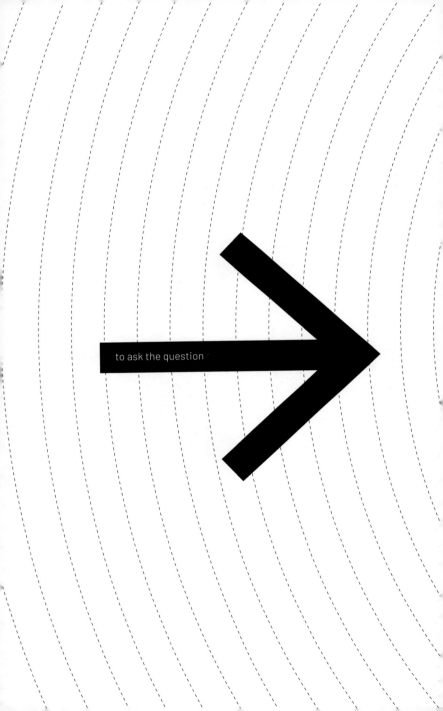

to ask the question

The answer to such questions is: your body will operate the way it's supposed to and you will live the life you're supposed to be living. The thinking mind isn't needed to live or to be happy. Only the working mind, flowing naturally and free of thoughts, is necessary. The working mind acts without a motive from the past or an expected future outcome (without doership). The working mind is the natural flow of pure consciousness.

Therefore the sage acts by not doing
and teaches no thought.
The ten thousand things arise
and vanish without him.
He works without motive,
indifferent to outcome.
Because there is no doer,
his actions are timeless.

~ *Tao Te Ching*, Marshall, Bart. (Tr), The Perennial Way, Tat Foundation

AFTERWORD

A PIECE OF TRUTH

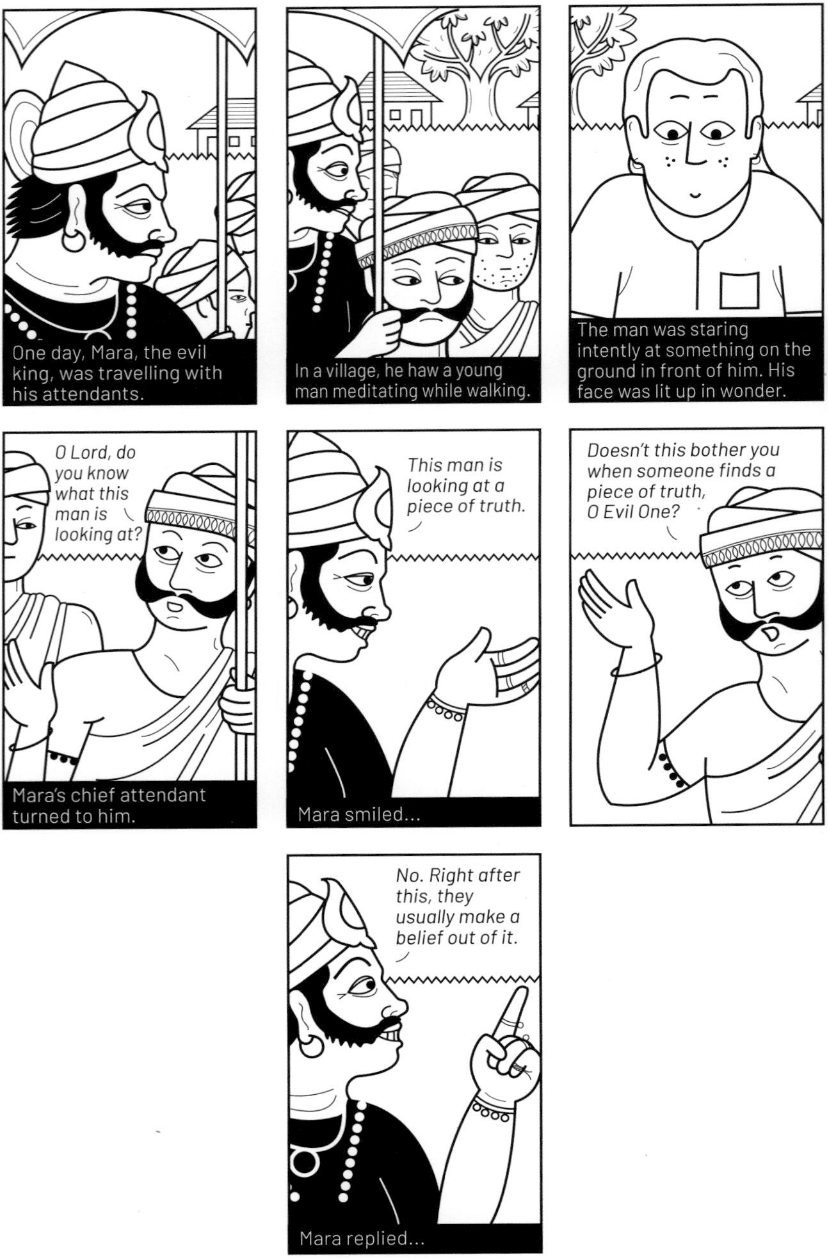
One day, Mara, the evil king, was travelling with his attendants.
In a village, he haw a young man meditating while walking.
The man was staring intently at something on the ground in front of him. His face was lit up in wonder.
O Lord, do you know what this man is looking at?
Mara's chief attendant turned to him.
This man is looking at a piece of truth.
Mara smiled...
Doesn't this bother you when someone finds a piece of truth, O Evil One?
No. Right after this, they usually make a belief out of it.
Mara replied...

The teachings in this book offer a 'piece of truth', but they are not meant to be believed blindly. The masters would want you to enquire and explore and experience for yourself instead of turning their words into a faith.

May Ramana and Ramesh's teachings act as a catalyst to your spiritual journey.

May your seeking bear fruit.

RECOMMENDED READING

Here's a reading list. Each one of these books is a spiritual classic. I would highly recommend that you read at least some of these.

Books on Ramana Maharshi's teachings

Maharshi, Ramana, *Who Am I?*, Sri Ramanasramam.

Maharshi, Ramana, Godman, David (Ed.), *Be As You Are: The spiritual teachings and wisdom of Sri Ramana Maharshi*. Penguin.

Maharshi, Ramana, Arthur Osborne (Ed.), *The Teachings of Sri Ramana Maharshi in His Own Words*. Sri Ramanasramam.

Balsekar, Ramesh, *Pointers From Ramana Maharshi*. Zen Publications.

Books on Ramesh Balsekar's teachings

Balsekar, Ramesh, *Consciousness Speaks*. Zen Publications.

Balsekar, Ramesh, *Confusion No More*. Zen Publications.

Sachdeva, Gautam, *Pointers from Ramesh Balsekar*. Yogi Impressions.

Other recommended reading

Marshall, Bart, *The Perennial Way: New English Versions of Yoga Sutras, Dhammapada, Heart Sutra, Astavakra Gita, Faith Mind Sutra, and Tao Te Ching*. Tat Foundation.

Prabhavananda, Swami, Isherwood, Christopher, *Bhagavad-Gita: The Song of God*. Penguin USA.

Prabhavananda, Swami, Isherwood, Christopher, *How to Know God: The Yoga Aphorisms of Patanjali*. Vedanta Press & Bookshop.

Sekida, Katsuki, *Two Zen Classics: The Gateless Gate and The Blue Cliff Records*. Shambhala.

Scientific research on how Genes and Conditioning influence decisions and choices.

Skinner, B. F, Beyond Freedom & Dignity, Hackett Publishing Co., 2011

Mitchell, Kevin J., *Innate: How the Wiring of Our Brains Shapes Who We Are.* Princeton University Press, 2018.

Tan, Monica, *Are we products of nature or nurture? Science answers age-old question.* The Guardian. May 2019.
https://www.theguardian.com/science/2015/may/19/are-we-products-of-nature-or-nuture-science-answers-age-old-question?CMP=share_btn_wa

Baggini, Julian, *Do your genes determine your entire life?* The Guardian. Mar 2019.
https://www.theguardian.com/science/2015/mar/19/do-your-genes-determine-your-entire-life?CMP=share_btn_wa

Harari, Yuval Noah, *The Myth of Freedom.* The Guardian. Sep 2018.
https://www.theguardian.com/books/2018/sep/14/yuval-noah-harari-the-new-threat-to-liberal-democracy

Scharping, Nathaniel, *Can We Blame Our Genes for Our Decisions?* Discover Magazine. December 2018.
https://www.discovermagazine.com/health/can-we-blame-our-genes-for-our-decisions

Acknowledgements

Siddharth would like to thank

Kalyani, her incredible talent made this book possible.

Parul, Arhaan, Vanashree, Mrugesh, Abhishek, Raghav, Anway, Ashwani, Arunima, Goutham, Mrugesh, and Sandy, for their encouragement and valuable feedback.

Nandita, she proofread this strange little thing and made it much better.

Gautam Sachdeva and David Godman, for their kindness and wise counsel.

Kalyani would like to thank

Siddharth, for trusting her with 'his baby' and giving her this amazing opportunity.

Gopika Chowfla, for her invaluable feedback and consistent support.

Aakancha, Sakshi, Shahana, Devshree, for always being there.

And her parents, for everything.

About the author

Siddharth Tripathi was born in Allahabad and schooled in Banaras. He is a BE from NIT Trichy and an MBA from MDI, Gurgaon. *The Virgins,* published in 2013, is his first novel. *Blowfish,* his second novel, was published by Bloomsbury in September 2017. His first two books are now being adapted for a serialized OTT release.

For the last five years, Siddharth has been a practitioner of the non-dual path to freedom and has extensively researched the Advaita teachings of Sri Ramana Maharshi and Sri Ramesh Balesekar. This book is a culmination of that journey.

About the illustrator

Kalyani S Naravane is a gold medallist from NIFT, New Delhi, with an MA in Illustration & Visual Media from LCC, UAL. She has completed five years as a graphic designer at GCD Studio, New Delhi. Kalyani is setting up her freelance practice, with the idea of integrating her love of illustrations and knowledge of graphic design in a challenging and creative way.